Vegan Indian COOKING

Vegan Indian COOKING

140 SIMPLE AND HEALTHY VEGAN RECIPES | *Anupy Singla*

S

SURREY
BOOKS

AN AGATE IMPRINT

CHICAGO

Printed in China.

All photographs copyright Brave New Pictures.
Design by Brandtner Design.

Library of Congress Cataloging-in-Publication Data

Singla, Anupy.
 Vegan Indian cooking : 140 simple and healthy vegan recipes / Anupy Singla.
    p. cm.
  ISBN 978-1-57284-130-7 (pbk.) -- ISBN 1-57284-130-3 (paperback) -- ISBN 978-1-57284-702-6 (ebook)
1. Cooking, Indic. 2. Vegan cooking. I. Title.
 TX724.5.I4S535 2012
 641.5'636--dc23
                    2012007435

12 13 14 15   10 9 8 7 6 5 4 3 2 1

Surrey Books is an imprint of Agate Publishing. Agate books are available in bulk at discount prices. For more information, go to agatepublishing.com.

This is for Neha and Aria, my beautiful girls
who are truly fearless in the kitchen.

Contents

Introduction

BEFORE I TELL YOU WHAT THIS BOOK IS, I WANT TO TELL YOU WHAT IT ISN'T. IT'S NOT a book that forces a lifestyle upon you. It's not a book that tells you what you should be eating on any given day. And it's most certainly not a book that insists I have all the answers. This is a book that tells you, "Eat what you want, but make sure what you eat is real, whole food. And open your mind to all of the possibilities."

This book is about those possibilities. The possibility of giving up meat for a meal, a day, a week, or a lifetime—whatever you choose. I grew up eating this way. My mother is a vegetarian who doesn't even eat eggs, but my father eats meat. In our home, we followed an Indian diet—which is predominantly vegetarian—most days. The only time we'd have meat would be for parties, when my mother would make chicken breast smothered in barbecue sauce, or when we'd make a rare run to a fast-food restaurant.

The way we ate then is the way a vast number of people still eat in India, where about 30 percent of the country's sizable population is vegetarian—primarily Hindus, Buddhists, and Jains. Most Muslims eat meat, just not pork; similarly, Hindus refrain from eating beef for religious reasons. (In India, even McDonald's is sensitive to local dietary restrictions and serves lamb burgers.)

This preference for vegetarian cuisine often has nothing to do with dairy products, a mainstay in Indian culture and cuisine. Thus, most Indians are lacto (milk) vegetarians. In my husband's childhood home (as in many households where meat is consumed), one day each week is observed as a holy day when no meat is eaten. On that day, his family would get their protein from *paneer*, a homemade cheese made from cow's milk. To this day, Tuesday is my husband's day to sit down to a meal of peas and homemade cheese (*mattar paneer*).

I first began my journey following a predominantly vegan diet (meaning no meat or dairy) back in the mid-1990s, when I was a graduate student at the East–West Center and the University of Hawaii. I fell ill with walking pneumonia and found that I had no energy. My immune system was shot. I went to see a naturopath, who suggested I give up milk, cheese, meat, and seafood for a period of six months so I could cleanse my system and better assess any possible food allergies.

Giving up the meat and seafood wasn't hard, but giving up dairy, on which I had been raised, was a challenge. I began to incorporate more soy milk and tofu into my diet, which wasn't a stretch because I already had grown to love both during the time I lived in Japan.

I quickly began to feel better and more energized, and I rarely got colds. I just felt healthier. I continued with this lifestyle change, but most importantly, I reverted to eating the foods my mother used to make when I was growing up in Pennsylvania: rice, beans, lentils, and lots of fresh vegetables. Mom was a true pioneer, one of the first Indians in America to use a slow cooker to make Indian food way back in the 1970s. I purchased a slow cooker and began to make all the Indian recipes she had developed in her slow cooker over the years.

The move to a vegan diet was relatively simple for me and made sense at the time, particularly since I personally do not like the taste of meat. Of course, that doesn't mean that your journey will be the same as mine. But I hope recipes from this book will encourage you to start thinking about incorporating more plant-based foods and simple, whole-food recipes into your daily diet.

I hope to fulfill two goals with this book. The first is to present you with everyday Indian recipes that are traditionally vegan. My Crackling Okra (see recipe on page 178), Tamarind Brown Rice (see recipe on page 196), and *Babaji's* Eggplant with Potatoes (see recipe on page 168) are just a few examples. If you grew up in a South Asian home, you'll recognize these recipes instantly, but some have my own twist on the traditional preparation. I've never cooked from an Indian cookbook, and I've only lately started using them as quick references as I write my own books. All of my experience cooking and eating Indian food comes from my own family (a bunch of foodies from Punjab) and my experiments working and studying in various home kitchens over the years.

My second goal is to give us South Asians a new way to think about the foods we grew up with. Just as in the West, life moves faster in Asia today, including India. As more and more women rightly enter the workforce, we have less time to cook the way our grandmothers and mothers did before us. (That's not to say men don't have a place in the kitchen. My grandfather directed the menu for

our family in India.) We are all desperately seeking shortcuts that preserve our sanity and get food on the table. In Indian grocery stores in India and beyond its borders, you'll find pre-packaged spice blends and food mixes, jarred chutneys, and frozen foods. You can easily stop at mainstream grocers and pick up a pouch of prepared Indian food and a bag of *naan* for a quick and seemingly healthy dinner for the family.

Always remember, though, that convenience has a price. These foods cook faster and are easier to prepare largely because they are processed and stripped of a majority of their nutrients to give you the quick dinner solution your mind, but not your body, craves. It might seem like it's always been the case—even in India—that Indian food is consumed with light, fluffy breads made from white flour and dishes concocted with premade spice mixtures. But it's simply not so. My mother still remembers her mother grinding whole wheat kernels into flour that would go into the hearty dinner *rotis* and roasting and grinding her own *garam masala* blend.

I want to preserve this history of whole-grain, wholesome cooking and add a new twist of convenience. In these pages, I'll show you how you can get the same level of nutrition and the same traditional flavors without a ton of added time and effort. Instead of using white rice to make tamarind rice, I've successfully made it with wholesome brown rice and even quinoa. Instead of giving you options for making *naan* (a type of leavened Indian bread typically made from processed white flour), I'll show you how to make *roti*, the whole-wheat bread that's really consumed on a daily basis in North Indian homes. *Dosas* pack a real nutritious punch when they are made with brown rice and

whole lentils instead of white rice and split and skinned lentils. Believe it or not, my kids actually request these whole-grain *dosas* every day.

Instead of heavy oils and unhealthy fats, I'll show you how to take simple ingredients, throw them into a slow cooker, and get mind-blowing results. While you are at work, the slow cooker will work its magic, infusing your key ingredients with spices and flavor, cooking lentils and beans to perfection, and allowing you to forgo unnecessary oils and dairy products.

One of my favorite sections in this book explains how you can easily cook batches of whole, dried beans and lentils in your slow cooker with nothing but water. The result: cooked legumes without added salt and other unhealthy additives that you can store in the refrigerator or freezer for a quick stovetop meal or a protein-rich addition to soups and salads. You won't have to waste your money or forgo taste and nutrition (yep—I said it!) with store-bought canned or frozen varieties ever again.

This book will also show you how these ingredients, mixed with the right spices, can become healing foods. Long a focal point of centuries-old Indian philosophy, spices are now being vigorously studied in the West—and rightly so—for their ability to help with not only common ailments but also serious diseases. One of the most exciting discoveries is that turmeric may contain elements that can help delay the onset of Alzheimer's disease.

Keep in mind that this book is not intended to be an anthology of Indian or vegan dishes. I prefer practicality over the wow factor. I didn't want to give you a five-hundred-recipe book that you would admire, but never actually open. I wanted, as I did with my last book, to give you recipes that you'll make over and over again. The recipes I present here will become favorites. They are the ones I feel comfortable saying I've perfected.

If you're already familiar with Indian cuisine, you'll wonder why some dishes didn't make it into this book. That's precisely why I love Indian food for a vegan or vegetarian diet—there really are that many options. As I tested recipe after recipe, the list of recipes I still wanted to try became longer and longer. But I had to stop somewhere and leave the additional recipes for my blog or future books, if I'm lucky enough to write more. So, enjoy what's here and know that there's more to come, including an amazing array of vegan and gluten-free desserts.

This is not a hands-free journey. I'm not saying that no work is required. You'll need to actively participate in this process. But know that I've done the research and testing needed to make it as painless as possible for you. Each recipe in this book was tested at least a dozen times, if not more. Many were sent to volunteer taste-testers around the country who became fans after using my first book, *The Indian Slow Cooker*. I have learned from everyone who has tested and tasted my food, tweaking each recipe where necessary.

All you have to do now is prepare to be open to any and all possibilities!

Getting Started

What in the World Is Vegan? Why Should I Consider It?

ANYONE WHO KNOWS ME WELL KNOWS THAT I LOATHE NEEDLESS FOOD LABELING. In the United States, it seems we've become more obsessed with differentiating our-selves at the expense of finding common ground. Why should it matter to me if you consider yourself a vegan but then eat out one Friday night and choose a meal with seafood in it? Why should it matter if are you a "less-devout" vegetarian who eats french fries cooked in oil derived from animal sources? I know my own answers to these questions, but they really only matter to me. I'm not worried about monitoring what you eat on a day-to-day basis.

My reluctance to label others likely results from a lifetime of being labeled myself. I grew up in a largely blue-collar community outside of Philadelphia and was teased from a young age about eating Indian food. "No way! Your house smells like curry," a little blonde girl down the street taunted when I suggested playing at my house. I still remember the awful feeling in my gut that her careless remark caused—like I'd been punched in the stomach.

I was also criticized for eating mostly vegetables. One friend invited me over to dinner only to have her mother (who was raised in south Philadelphia) ask, "But what do I serve her? She does eat chicken, right? Vegetarians eat chicken, don't they?"

Then there were the meat-obsessed Indian friends I encountered after I got married and moved to Chicago. "You really don't eat meat? But you grew up in America. Why would you give up meat? Can't you just pick it out?"

And there were the endless years of attending work Christmas parties with my husband, whose former boss and his wife would insist on serving meat dishes almost exclusively, even though they knew my dietary restrictions. Even my one safe haven (the salad) always had bacon sprinkled on it.

Enough already!

To me, labels are not tools for judging what others can and cannot do on a daily basis. Instead, they're merely a way to understand a person's food philosophy and thus fine-tune my suggestions on food when I dine out with them or invite them to my house for a meal. For this reason, I think it's a good idea to understand the variety of food labels and culinary choices out there, especially in the nonmeat-eating world.

- **VEGETARIAN:** A general term that describes anyone who follows a plant-based diet. Veg-etarians do not eat red meat, seafood, or poultry. Some eat dairy and eggs, while others do not.

- **LACTO-OVO VEGETARIAN:** A vegetarian who eats dairy products and eggs.
- **LACTO VEGETARIAN:** A vegetarian who eats dairy products but not eggs. Most Indians fall into this category.
- **VEGAN:** A vegetarian who does not eat dairy, eggs, or any product derived from animal products. Some vegans also abstain from eating honey harvested from bees, gelatin (made from animals), and processed sugars (some of which have been filtered through bone char, which is made from burnt animal bones).

Why Indian Cuisine Is a Natural Choice for Anyone on a Vegan Diet

One beautiful day many years ago, when my friend Anuj and I were graduate students in Hawaii, we drove to our favorite spot on the windward side of Oahu for a swim with one of his friends. There in Kailua, the water is so clear you can see your toes curled in the white, silky sand below.

I sat on the beach and watched our friend bobbing in the water, horrified. He actually glowed orange against the blue-greens of the ocean! When I asked him later about his noticeable color change, I learned that he had recently become a vegan and was eating about a pound of carrots and a dozen or so papaya a day. I was completely shocked that he would think this was in any way, shape, or form a healthy way to eat—let alone thrive.

My whole life, I have listened to non-Indian friends and strangers talk about their forays toward vegetarianism and cite a common struggle—figuring out what to eat besides salad and steamed vegetables. I'm here to tell you that there's a whole cuisine for you!

Because I grew up eating Indian food, I never had this problem. As I kept busy working and studying through the years, I could never really put my finger on why. One day, it hit me. Indian food is the only major cuisine in which vegetables take center stage.

Think about that. You can't say the same about any other cuisine—Italian, Mexican, Greek, Spanish, or Chinese. In every one of them, red meat, seafood, or poultry take the limelight, and while vegetable dishes are part of the repertoire, they are often used to help showcase the main nonvegetarian culinary event. Even a broth soup with vegetables is generally flavored with meat.

The vegetarian-focused way of Indian cuisine has developed over the course of centuries and is rooted in religion. As Hinduism, Buddhism, and certain other religions became prevalent on the Indian subcontinent, so did the idea of *ahimsa*, or nonviolence. This idea of nonviolence crossed over from daily actions to include actions associated with eating. Hindus and followers of other religions—especially in India—believe animals should also be protected by *ahimsa*.

Because of this strong focus on vegetarianism, legumes such as beans and lentils and grains are a key source of nutrients and protein in the Indian diet. If you say to most any Indian that you need meat to get protein, he or she will likely laugh at you. It's just not the case. Any Indian can cite hundreds upon hundreds of vegetarian dishes and preparations—most of them vegan.

Indian food is also a natural choice these days for those with food allergies. I'm frequently contacted by people who have a sensitivity or intolerance to gluten (the binding "glue" in wheat that creates havoc for some, especially those with celiac disease). They are usually joyful emails about discovering Indian cuisine. In North Indian cooking, gluten is found only in breads and some desserts. These breads can easily be made gluten free by switching to a nonwheat flour, which I often do during kids' cooking classes that I teach in Chicago. I encourage those who are gluten-sensitive or gluten-intolerant to try South Indian breads (*dosas*), which are made from rice and lentils.

Take note: if you have allergies or are sensitive to certain foods, always consider the source when shopping for ingredients. Though an ingredient like chickpea flour (*besan*) may be naturally gluten free, the facility where it is processed may not be. Thus, the flour could be harmful. Purchase your ingredients from a source you trust, and make sure the label indicates that it is gluten free.

Even if you do not generally follow a vegan diet and are allergy free, you will still love these traditional and wholesome recipes.

Indian Food Myths

Misconceptions about Indian food run rampant. This is especially true outside metropolitan areas, where exposure to Indian cuisine and spices is less common. During my many instances of writing for various news publications and the cooking demonstrations I've taken part in across this continent over the past year, I've been on a mission to demystify the whole concept of Indian food and cooking. There are a few key misconceptions that still need to be addressed.

- **INDIAN FOOD IS SPICY.** It truly doesn't have to be—especially if you cook it at home, where you have control over the ingredients. Spices impart flavor to your dishes, and flavor does not necessarily mean heat. The only ingredients that can give your dish heat are fresh green chiles, dried whole red chiles, and red chile powder. If you don't like heat or are afraid of it, just use less of these three ingredients.
- **INDIAN FOOD IS COMPLICATED.** Not at all. Actually preparing the dishes is not complicated or difficult. Other than initially assembling your spices, the only hurdle is serving the meal. Most meals include one or two main dishes and a few sides, such as a simple cucumber and onion salad, an Indian pickle (*achaar*), and chutney. The key to a good Indian food experience is having sweet, savory, spicy, soft, and crunchy foods all on the same plate. Most nights, my mother managed to whip up meals in minutes and get us to the table relatively quickly. With Indian cuisine, it's all in the prep and the planning.
- **INDIAN FOOD IS UNHEALTHY AND HEAVY.** Homestyle Indian is anything but heavy. In this respect, Indian restaurants in the West have given Indian food a bad reputation. Most restaurants dump a ton of cream and oil into their dishes, thinking that's what their customers want. In fact, this prevents you from tasting the food. Sure, it seems delicious while you are eating it. But afterward, you feel bloated and slightly uncomfortable—and let's not mention how you feel the next morning! Indian food should be light, delicious, and fresh. When I taught a class at a Sur La Table in King of Prussia, Pennsylvania, one participant remarked he'd never liked okra in the past but loved it the way I made it because he could actually taste the vegetable.
- **INDIANS EAT *NAAN*.** Well, we do now. But growing up, I never ate *naan* except when we ate at an Indian restaurant. *Naan* is a leavened bread made of processed white flour and cooked in a *tandoor* (clay oven). No one I know in India or in the States owns an oven like this. The daily bread of choice in Indian homes is *roti*, which is also called *chapati* or *phulka*. Like a tortilla, it's an unleavened bread made on the stovetop. It's healthy, delicious, and less fattening than *naan*. The main reason *naan* has overshadowed *roti* is because of Indian restaurants, which always like to showcase their tandoors and, of course, the *naan* that comes out of them. Next time you're in an Indian restaurant, ask for *tandoori roti*. It's a whole-wheat *roti* puffed up in a *tandoor*—as delicious as *naan* but made from healthier whole grains.

- **THE SLOW COOKER ISN'T INDIAN.** The concept of slow cooking began in India well before the first slow cooker went on the market in the United States. *Dum Pukht*, or slow oven cooking, is a technique that began about two centuries ago in Awadh, India. It involves placing foods, including meats, rice, and spices, in a container over a very low flame. The pot is then sealed with wet flour so that no steam can escape during the cooking process. Many hours later, the dough seal is broken and the slow-cooked magnificence of the flavors and spices can be enjoyed as a one-pot meal. Sound familiar? In many ways, this is the precursor to the American slow cooker! When I tested my recipes for *The Indian Slow Cooker*, I found that spices placed in the slow cooker—even without being toasted—and cooked for hours at a time provide the same flavor that they would if they had been toasted the traditional way: heated in oil on the stovetop before adding them to a dish. Try it—you'll be convinced! My mother was one of the first in this country to extensively use slow cookers to make Indian food. Most South Asians still use a pressure cooker, which compresses and locks in steam to cook ingredients very rapidly. While this can be a last-minute time saver, many of the younger set of the Indian community have seen our mothers' pressure cookers blow up. Thus, we're reluctant to use them, even the safer versions now on the market. The quick-cooking method of the pressure cooker also does not allow the flavors to meld, break down, and truly infuse the food. While pressure cooking is incredibly handy, with a little planning, you can achieve a tastier product with a slow cooker. However, there is no one way to cook. Every day can be different. I like to give my readers as many options as possible so they can decide what works for them on any given day or week. Slow cookers have not taken off in India simply because pressure cookers are used so extensively and because electricity is not always reliable. (If you are preparing a meal in a slow cooker and the electricity gets cut off for any reason, your food will spoil.) My *Mattu Massi* (maternal aunt) in Chandigarh cooked extensively with a slow cooker when visiting England recently and was so impressed by it that she purchased one for every family member in India. It's a concept that still might take off there.

- **CURRY POWDER IS A KEY INDIAN SPICE.** Would you be floored if I told you I've never used curry powder for Indian cooking? It's not a traditional Indian spice; rather, it's a blend that British folks who had spent time in India created to mimic the tastes and smells of Indian food. Curry powder has become a popular ingredient in Japan (for their curried rice), Singapore, and parts of Malaysia. Indian grocery stores sell it, and some Indian households use it, but it's not a part of traditional dishes and cooking. To clarify, the word *curry* is used in India, but it is used generally to refer to a dish that has a broth, such as a chicken curry. *Sabji* refers to a dry dish, such as cauliflower and potatoes (*aloo gobi*).

- **INDIAN FOOD DOESN'T REQUIRE MEASUREMENTS.** Most of my family cooks without measuring—but these folks have been cooking Indian food all their lives. For most of the rest of us (including me, when a recipe is new), measurements help. Indian food is incredibly forgiving—if you add a 1½-inch (3.8-cm) piece of ginger root rather than a 1-inch (2.5-cm) piece, it's no biggie. But when you start out, I believe precision will make you more confident. That's why in this book, I indicate that a medium tomato, diced, measured out to be a cup for me. For you, it might be a little more or a little less. It doesn't matter much, but at least you know what I used. I don't want measurements to hold you back from being creative; instead, I want you to see them as a foundation to build upon as you become more comfortable with the recipes.

Indian Spices 102

My last book included a primer on Indian spices (Indian Spices 101). I've included all that information and more in this book, so it's Indian Spices 102!

It may surprise you to learn this, but spices don't just look and smell nice. They also have many health benefits. Indians have known this for centuries, and they use common spices to cure everything from a cough to a stomachache and even to help heal broken bones.

In our home, my young girls know to ask for turmeric-and-black-cardamom-spiced *chai* (tea) if they're home from school with a cold. Whenever she coughs, even a little, my Aria asks for ginger juice with lemon and honey. If I have a fever or stuffy nose, my eldest daughter, Neha, quickly grabs the garlic press and has me take a minced clove with water.

Even at their young ages, my girls realize and feel the very real effects of these home remedies. What they don't realize now, but will later in life, is that all the spices included in their foods on a daily basis will also help with the big stuff—supporting their immune systems and helping them fight off everything from diabetes to heart disease. Spices can do it all.

Don't get me wrong. Including spices in your diet is not like taking a magic pill, and they don't work overnight. They work slowly and over time as anti-inflammatory agents. As such, they've been proven to help ward off many types of illnesses. Nothing is ever a sure bet, but why not try to control what you can control, and slowly start incorporating spices into your daily menu? It's so easy to do—especially when you have a book like this to help you learn.

The first thing I emphasize in the classes I teach is that although hundreds of spices and spice blends are available, you shouldn't feel intimidated. You don't need them all. Essentially, you need

only seven or eight basic spices to get started, and a few more to take it to the next level. Most seemingly complicated blends of spices can be made from these basic starter spices, with a few additions.

These basic spices include cumin seeds (for North Indian cooking), mustard seeds (for South Indian cooking), turmeric powder, ground coriander, *garam masala* (a blend of spices used in North Indian cooking), and red chile powder. I also like to keep coarse white sea salt and black salt (*kala namak*) on hand for general flavoring and for making Indian side salads. These were the primary spices my mother used in her own cooking.

Don't worry if you don't like spicy food—Indian is still for you. Spices don't equal heat; instead, they equal flavor. Many people have told me that they've avoided Indian food because they've assumed it was spicy. Once they try my food, they're usually converted. The only heat providers in Indian cooking are fresh green chiles, whole dried red chiles, or red chile powder. Reduce or eliminate them, and you're still left with an incredibly flavorful and well-seasoned meal.

I'm often asked how to store spices and for how long they remain useful. In their whole form, spices can last for years. But once they're ground, their essential oils are released. Because of that, you'll be able to keep them in ground form for six months, tops, before they go rancid and lose their flavor. This is why most people who really understand spices and have worked with them purchase most spices whole and grind their own on an as-needed basis. In these pages, I'll show you how you can do this for yourself. It's easy and likely will save you money in the long run.

To keep your spices fresh, make sure they never get wet. Always use a clean, completely dry spoon to measure out your spices, and store them in a cool, dry space in your kitchen.

Spices should be kept in glass jars or stainless steel containers. I purchase many of my spices in large quantities (since I know I'll get through them), which I store in stacking containers in a cabinet. I keep the spices I use most frequently in a traditional Indian spice box made of stainless steel: the *masala dabba*. It stays on my counter, easy to grab whenever I need it.

The *masala dabba* is the quintessential tool in the Indian kitchen. It's a round stainless steel container with seven small, round stainless steel containers inside. Each small container holds a single essential spice and can be removed so that you can measure out its spice right into any dish you are making.

While I was testing recipes for my first book, I grew increasingly frustrated that most traditional *masala dabbas* did not allow the user to level a teaspoon, tablespoon, or any other measuring spoon directly in the container. I knew this was an opportunity, so I traveled to India and found a manufacturer for my very own patent-pending design—an updated version of the traditional *masala dabba* with standard measuring spoons that fit right into the box. Williams-Sonoma started selling my version of the *dabba* in 2011 (see photo on page 25), and it's also available on my website, www.indianASapplepie.com.

The following list is not meant to be a complete anthology of Indian spices; instead, it's a comprehensive reference for the spices used in this cookbook, which also happen to be the most frequently used spices in Indian food.

- **AMLA:** Also known as Indian gooseberry, *nellikai*, and *emblica*, amla is a round, pale greenish-yellow-colored fruit that is about the size of a golf ball and extremely tart when eaten fresh. The back yard of my mother's childhood home in Chandigarh has two *amla* trees that are harvested to this day for the versatile and therapeutic fruit. One of the richest natural sources of Vitamin C, *amla* is typically sold in Indian grocery stores in dried form and cut into small pieces. It may also be shredded or whole, black in color, and shriveled. It takes about two hours of soaking in hot water to reconstitute dried *amla*. I often soak a few pieces of *amla*, along with a little turmeric and lemon juice, for about 10 minutes in a cup of extremely hot water and drink it as a cleanser in the morning before I eat or drink anything else. Frozen, whole *amla*

MASALA DABBA

1. Black Mustard Seeds
2. Cardamom and
   Cinnamon Sticks
3. Coriander Seeds
4. Turmeric Powder
5. Cumin Seeds
6. Sea Salt
7. Red Chile Powder

can also be found; once you defrost it, eat it with a little black salt or blend it into a smoothie. The best way to use *amla* in your dishes is to add about a half-dozen dried pieces to the lentil and bean recipes featured in the Slow-Cooked Legumes to Stovetop section. You'll infuse them with a rich, healthy dose of Vitamin C; enhance their flavor; and add a little sourness, which always works well in Indian dishes. Be sure to carefully monitor the salt level in your dish if you can only find dried and salted *amla*, but it likely won't make too much difference in the final dish. *Amla* is also used to make many cosmetic products, including hair oils and face masks. I've used *amla* oil for years to help untangle my younger daughter's wild, curly hair.

- **ASAFETIDA (ASAFOETIDA, HING):** Also known as *devil's dung*, asafetida is quite fragrant and incredibly pungent. It is collected from the large roots of a tall, smelly herb as a resin-like gum that is then dried and sold in solid lumps or as a powder. Uncooked, asafetida has a strong, overpowering smell, so it should always be stored in an airtight container. The key to using asafetida is to add a little bit to heated oil in order to break it down before you mix it in with your dish. Asafetida is believed to aid digestion and to help prevent gas, especially when used in bean and lentil dishes. Don't worry about the smell—it goes away as it's cooked, leaving you with a warm, even flavor that tastes a bit like leeks to balance out your dishes. You just need a pinch, because a little goes a long way.

- **BLACK SALT (KALA NAMAK):** Hands down my favorite spice, *kala namak* is mined from soft-stone quarries in northern India and Pakistan. Its name clearly implies a black color, but the color of this condiment actually ranges from a brownish-pink to a dark violet when it is mined and then light purple to pink once it is ground to a powder. *Kala namak* is mainly sodium chloride, but it is also rich in trace minerals, including magnesium and volcanic iron. When used with fresh ingredients, such as vegetables, yogurts, and lentils, it enhances the foods' natural taste and gives you a pop of flavor. Its sulfuric tones make it a perfect addition to my *Masala* Tofu Scramble, as it imparts the smell and taste of eggs. Some believe that black salt does not increase the sodium content of the blood in the way that white salt does, so it is often recommended for people with high blood pressure or who are on low-sodium diets. It also helps alleviate indigestion and heartburn. My kids can never resist fresh, crunchy veggies doused with lemon juice and sprinkled with *kala namak*.

- **CARDAMOM (ELAICHI):** Known as the queen of spices, green (*hara*) cardamom typically grows in southern India as pods on a six-foot-tall shrub. One of the most valued and costliest spices in the world, it contains twenty-five volatile oils. Key among these is *cineole*, which is also found in bay leaves. *Cineole* is being studied for its many benefits, which include aiding digestion, getting rid of bad breath, inhibiting the growth of ulcers, and preventing colon cancer. It's the primary flavor in traditional Indian tea, well-spiced basmati rice, meat stews, and desserts like *kheer*. White cardamom is just green cardamom that has been chemically bleached. It's used in Eastern European baking and in sauces where the color needs to be maintained.

Black or brown cardamom (*kali* or *bardi elaichi*) is a large, woody-looking pod that is used in India to spice rice and meat dishes. I love its flavor in some of my lentil dishes, and I like to use it in my *chai masala* to help stifle a cough. Although the medicinal properties of black cardamom still need further research, my mother-in-law firmly believes that it helps prevent coughing. In my own experience, I've found that to be consistently true.

- **CAROM SEEDS (AJWAIN, AJOWAN):** These small, pungent seeds come from an annual shrub from the same family as cumin and caraway, and they carry a powerful punch. Small and light brown, they look like cumin (*jeera*) but have a much more distinct flavor. They are used to flavor breads, lentil dishes such as *kitchari*, snacks made from gram (chickpea) flour (*besan*), and biscuits. A few tablespoons of water boiled with these seeds are usually enough to ease an upset stomach, gas, or diarrhea. Try chewing on the seeds raw, and you'll feel the results immediately—a flood of warm bitterness and a slightly numbing effect from the thymol in the seeds. Researchers believe the presence of choline in *ajwain* is what helps soothe the digestive tract.

- **CASSIA LEAVES (TEJ PATTA):** Often mistaken for bay leaves, cassia leaves are also referred to as Indian bay leaves. They are large, often five to eight inches long (I measured them!) and come from a tropical laurel that produces cassia bark. They are thin, brittle, and a dull beige in color. At once woodsy, pungent, and sweet, they have a very different taste and aroma from the more common bay leaf, which comes from a different tree and is used in European cooking. If you cannot get to an Indian grocery store for cassia leaves, just use bay leaves. No one will know the difference—I cook with both.

- **CHILE:** The chile pepper was discovered in the Americas by Christopher Columbus, whose quest, as you might remember, was to find spices in India. It has since become one of the most widely consumed spices in the world, with many varieties, shapes, colors, and applications. Chiles derive their heat and healing properties from capsaicin, an alkaloid found mostly in the seeds and inner membranes of chiles. This substance has been shown to boost metabolism, prevent blood clots, and improve cholesterol, among other benefits. Its ability to kill off tumor cells in test animals and human cell cultures is also being studied. This cookbook gives you a range of chiles that are ideal for use in Indian cooking, from the tiny but very spicy Thai chile to the longer serrano and cayenne chiles. In my home, we use Thai chiles, and we use the maxi-

mum amount listed in each recipe of this book. I want to be honest here—we have a household that loves heat. But use your common sense when using chiles for yourself. If you can't handle heat, use the amount at the bottom of the suggested range or omit the chiles altogether. You can also remove the membrane and seeds (using kitchen gloves), which harbor the capsaicin, in order to manage the heat while keeping the flavor. Whole dried red chiles (*sabut lal mirch*) are used extensively in Indian cooking and in this book to make spice blends and round out curries. These can range in color from light to deep red and even black, depending on the variety of the chile used and the region it is from. There are thick, long chiles as well as short, round ones. Most taste the same with slight variations in flavor. When I write about red chile powder (*lal mirch*), I am referring to the powdered chiles found in bags in Indian grocery stores.

If you can't get to an Indian grocer, use cayenne, which is the same thing. However, I find that chile powder from Indian groceries packs a little more heat. Don't mistake it for Mexican chili powder, which is generally used to make American chili and is sometimes mixed with salt and other spices, including cumin, to make Indian chile powder.

- **PAPRIKA (*DEGHI MIRCH*):** Paprika is made from dried sweet peppers from Kashmir. This powder is used to give curries a reddish color without adding heat.
- **CINNAMON (*DALCHINI*):** Cinnamon is derived from the inner bark of the upper branches of a tree native to Sri Lanka, the largest supplier of this spice in the world. In Indian cooking, cinnamon is not just reserved for dessert. It is primarily used to subtly spice savory dishes, including quick vegetable stir fries, rice, and even more elaborate curries. It has myriad health

benefits, including the ability to help manage blood sugar. I purchase my cinnamon in sticks and use it whole. Before grinding cinnamon to make a spice blend, I recommend breaking the sticks up. The best way to do so is to wrap them in a clean dishcloth and lightly pound on the sticks with a meat tenderizer or heavy tool until they are broken into small pieces—obviously taking care not to damage your counter.

- **CLOVE (LAUNG):** Cloves are the dried, unopened flower buds of a tropical evergreen. They grow in small clusters and are small and brown with bumpy ends. They are used to subtly spice rice dishes, curries, desserts, and *chai*. The key to using this spice effectively is in knowing how strong its taste can be. The most experienced Indian cooks know to use it sparingly. It's no secret that the essential oil in cloves, eugenol, is used to help ease the pain from toothaches. The last time I was at the dentist, he used clove oil to help ease the pain and numb the working area.

- **CORIANDER SEEDS (SABUT DHANIYA):** Coriander is the seed, and the plant (herb) is called cilantro. These green-yellow, grassy seeds impart a wonderful and subtle lemony taste to a dish. The seeds are used in various spice blends, dry roasted, or heated in oil to release their essential oils. Coriander can be purchased already ground or can be easily ground at home with either a coffee grinder reserved for spices or a simple mortar and pestle. Coriander seeds are very good for you (more so than cilantro). Coriander tea helps relieve stomachaches, while the seeds have been shown to decrease blood sugar levels and increase insulin output—good news for those who suffer from diabetes.

- **CUMIN SEEDS (JEERA):** Cumin seeds are an essential spice in Indian cuisine, especially in the north. The small, beige seeds seem relatively dull and boring on their own, but heat them in oil and the result is what memories are made of—a flavor that is at once warm, comforting, and embracing. The beauty of this little seed is not just in its culinary flavoring, but in its health properties. In scientific studies, cumin has been shown to fight diabetes and cancerous tumors, and it may help prevent bone loss. This little seed also packs a mean nutritious punch.

- **ROASTED CUMIN (BHUNA HUA JEERA):** I love getting double duty from my spices. Dry roast your cumin and grind it in a coffee grinder reserved for spices. (Yes, you can purchase roasted cumin, but if you roast and grind it yourself, you'll taste a world of difference.) Use it in your soy yogurt *raitas* and even in soups and stews.

- **CURRY LEAVES (KARI PATTA):** Curry leaves have nothing to do with curry powder. The leaves are synonymous with South Indian cuisine and are to that region what cilantro is to North Indian cooking—omnipresent. Grown on a tree that's a member of the citrus family, the curry leaf is sold in Indian grocery stores still attached to thin, wiry branches. Pull the leaves off and throw them into hot oil and you'll suddenly release all of the essential oils and flavors—an addictive deep and grassy taste, kind of a cross between lemongrass and tangerines, and virtually indescribable. The fresh leaves are best; dried or frozen, they lose flavor.

- **FENNEL SEEDS (SAUNF):** These tiny seeds, which look like slightly curled green cumin, are the dried seeds from the yellow flowers of a large, dill-like perennial plant. They have a light, licorice-type taste and are used to help digestion and freshen breath. Whenever you leave an Indian restaurant, take a spoonful of *saunf* from the little bowl at the door to help freshen your breath and digest your meal. The seeds are used in everything from *chai* to meat dishes. Dry roast them for a mellower flavor.

- **FENUGREEK SEEDS (METHI DANA):** Small, hard, and square, these beige seeds are powerful in terms of taste and nutrition. Derived from the pods of the fenugreek plant, the seeds are legumes. The slightly bitter taste adds the complex combination of sweet and sour to many dishes, including my Sweet and Sour Sweet Potatoes (see recipe on page 182). The key is to be careful when frying the seeds in oil. Take them off the heat when they get reddish brown; any darker and they become so bitter that they are virtually inedible. Fenugreek seeds are also medicinal, with research showing that they have the ability to regulate blood sugar levels and help control diabetes. Grind this spice and add it to your dishes, or do as many in India do: sprout the seeds (see page 111) and add them to a soup or salad. Fenugreek leaves (*kasoori methi*) are also used extensively in Indian cooking. These are the dried leaves of the fenugreek plant, which has yellow and white flowers and resembles alfalfa. Add a small handful of these leaves to a curry or to breads, and you'll be pleasantly surprised by the added layers of flavor. The key when using the leaves is to first crush them slightly in your hand to release their flavor. Fresh fenugreek leaves are also found in the produce section of most well-stocked Indian grocery stores and can be chopped and mixed into potato or other Indian stir-fry dishes.

CUMIN SEEDS

GROUND CUMIN

ROASTED GROUND CUMIN

FENUGREEK SEEDS

CLOVES

CORIANDER SEEDS

GROUND CORIANDER

BLACK MUSTARD SEEDS

TURMERIC POWDER

BLACK SALT/*KALA NAMAK*

GARAM MASALA

GREEN CARDAMOM

- **GINGER (GROUND):** This powdered form of the ginger root is useful to keep on hand if you don't have fresh ginger root or for spicing *chai* and stir-fry dishes.
- **MANGO POWDER (*AMCHUR*):** This tart, beige powder is made from uncooked, dried, unripe, and green mangoes. It is delicious sprinkled on Indian snack foods and in dishes such as Crackling Okra (see recipe on page 178), Cumin Potato Hash (see recipe on page 162), and Chickpea Flour Curry with Veggies (see recipe on page 162). In terms of taste, it functions like lemon juice or vinegar and is usually added toward the end of the cooking process.
- **MASALA:** By definition, a *masala* is simply a blend. Remember that movie *Mississippi Masala*? It was about an Indian girl dating an African-American guy—a mix of cultures. Get it now? There are dozens upon dozens of *masalas* out there, so a cook can grab the appropriate one for his or her dish instead of adding each individual ingredient. These spice blends differ by type and amount of individual spices. The blends can be purchased, but they are just as easy to make at home. Try it, and you might be pleasantly surprised. *Chai masala* is the standard blend of cardamom, cloves, and cinnamon that gives Indian tea its unique flavor and warm smell. *Chaat masala*, which is uniquely tart and highly addictive, flavors many street foods called *chaat*. Its key ingredients include mango powder and black salt. Sprinkle a little over fresh veggies along with some lemon juice, and you'll see just how addictive it is for adults and kids alike. *Chana masala* includes pomegranate seeds, fenugreek, and mustard seeds, among other spices, which combine to give this blend its unique tartness. It's traditionally cooked with chickpeas but can be used in virtually any dish. Chutney powder is a tart, reddish-pink powder sprinkled over fresh *dosas* in South Indian cooking. Because it's used so infrequently, I did not include a recipe in my book. It can be found at any Indian grocery store. *Garam masala* is synonymous with North Indian cooking. This spice blend includes cumin, coriander seeds, and cassia leaves, among other ingredients. It's a classic way to quickly cook up a standard North Indian curry. *Rasam masala* (powder), used to flavor the classic South Indian soup by the same name, combines lentils and curry leaves with spices to get its unique flavor. *Sambhar masala*, a delicious and fiery combination of lentils, curry leaves, spices, and whole red chiles, flavors South Indian *sambhar* stew but can be used in other soups and lentil dishes as well as sprinkled over popcorn.

- **MUSTARD SEEDS (RAI):** These tiny, hard, round seeds are to South Indian cooking what cumin seeds are to North Indian cuisine. They are usually added to hot oil and popped for a quick tempering for stir-fry dishes and stews. They are also used in everything from salads to lentil stews to pickles. Ground to a powder, they can add tartness to a dish, and when ground to a paste, they provide a mustard taste. The seeds come from the mustard plant, which is a cruciferous plant—in the same cancer-fighting plant family as broccoli, Brussels sprouts, cabbage, and kale. The tiny mustard seed contains the same compounds in concentrated form. There are yellow, brown, and black mustard seeds. The yellow is used to make American mustard; the brown is popular in Europe and Asia; and the black, which is the smallest and most potent of the three, is used most often in Indian cooking and pressed to make mustard oil. All come from different varieties of the mustard plant and can be used interchangeably.

- **NIGELLA SEEDS (KALONJI):** These tiny black seeds are the product of an annual flowering plant. The seeds are sometimes referred to as onion seeds or black cumin, but they are related to neither. They do, when sizzled in hot oil, taste a bit like onions and look like onion seeds—hence the incorrect reference. They are used in curries, added to Indian pickles (*achaar*), and used to top Indian breads, including *naan*.

- **NUTMEG (JAIPHAL):** This spice is actually the seed of an evergreen tree, and the spice known as mace is the covering of this seed. Nutmeg can be purchased whole, in which case it is slightly wrinkled and beige-brown. It can also be purchased as a pre-ground powder. It's not used extensively in Indian cooking, but my family uses it in our *garam masala* recipe.

- **POMEGRANATE SEEDS (DRIED) (ANARDANA):** From a wild Indian pomegranate, these seeds are dried and used to add sourness to various dishes and *masala* blends, including *chana masala*. They are sold as whole, sticky seeds and in powder form. The pomegranate fruit and its juice have become trendy as a healthy food source, primarily because of the large number of polyphenols, which are disease-fighting antioxidants found in plants, that they contain. Whether fresh, dried, or as a juice, this is one fruit to add to your daily routine.

- **TURMERIC POWDER (HALDI):** If there is one spice my family cannot do without, it's turmeric. Derived from a root, like ginger, it grows in the ground and is washed, peeled, dried, and ground into the bright yellow-orange powder you likely know. A staple in Indian cooking and religious ceremonies (brides are washed in turmeric as part of their prewedding beauty regimen), this magic powder is a natural antibacterial agent. Its active ingredient, curcumin, is currently being studied for its ability to combat serious diseases, including cancer and Alzheimer's disease. My girls know to ask for a little turmeric when they cut themselves. We gargle with it when we have sore throats, and we layer it in fresh Indian breads when we have colds. Its uses are endless and amazing, but don't get it near your clothes. The yellow stains will last forever! (I still have stains on my favorite outfit from my cousin Vikram's wedding.) At some specialty Indian grocers, you can find turmeric fresh, whole, and in yellow and white forms. Grab it, peel it, and grate it into your favorite salads.

- **WHITE SALT (NAMAK):** Basic white salt is used extensively in Indian cooking to enhance flavor and balance dishes. I use coarse sea salt. If you use regular table salt (which has smaller crystals), use half the amount of salt called for in my recipes. Salt levels are very personal, and they can differ quite a bit among cooks and their families. In my household, we rarely, if ever, eat processed or canned foods, which are the biggest sources of hidden salts. Because of this, I can be slightly more liberal with the amount of salt I use in my cooking. You may have a different routine and different needs. Feel free to tweak the salt levels in my recipes to suit your palate.

For more information on spices, their health benefits, and where to find them, check out the following two fantastic books:

- *Healing Spices: How to Use 50 Everyday and Exotic Spices to Boost Health and Beat Disease* by Bharat B. Aggarwal and Debora Yost
- *The Indian Grocery Store Demystified* by Linda Bladholm

My Vegan Indian Pantry

You'll always be able to cook up a delicious Indian meal if you keep certain key ingredients on hand. Cooking without meat and animal products is just as easy. Giving up animal-based products has become painless with the plethora of products now available on grocery store shelves. This list will give you an idea of the most popular ingredient substitutes and ones I use regularly. New ingredients are introduced almost daily, so use this list as a guide and add to it as you go on your own culinary journey.

For the sake of full disclosure, I must add my feelings on processed foods here. So many ingredients now are rigged to taste and feel like meat. I use some of them in my cooking. However, I never encourage making processed food a significant part of your diet. Whether you eat meat or maintain a meat-free diet, processed foods should be "sometimes," not "always," foods. If you read the labels on veggie sausages and some meat-substitute crumbles, you'll be shocked to see how much salt they contain. You don't have to eliminate these items entirely, but use them only to enhance your key ingredients: fresh fruit and veggies, beans, lentils, and grains.

- **BUTTER:** When you adopt a vegan lifestyle and diet, butter might at first seem difficult to replace. These days, it's a cinch. Earth Balance and Spectrum offer vegan margarine in tubs and in stick form. If you are soy sensitive, be careful to read all packaging on margarine and other butter alternatives. Many of these products are made with soy, but some companies are introducing soy-free alternatives that use olive and coconut oils instead. The only drawback to the coconut spread is that it tastes like coconut—not a flavor I like to combine with all my foods. The soy and olive oil spreads are more neutral.

- **CILANTRO (DHANIYA):** This herb is used extensively in Indian cooking, especially in the north. It has little nutritional value (unlike its seed, coriander), but it adds incredible flavor to a dish. It can take a pretty good dish to perfectly heavenly in seconds. Chop the leaves and the tender parts of the stem and sprinkle them over your dishes toward the end of cooking. I also like to use it ground into a paste to infuse my slow-cooked beans and lentils with incredible flavor.

- **COCONUT (NARIAL, NARIYAL):** What we know as the white, fleshy coconut is actually the interior nut of the large, brown, and hairy fruit of coconut palm trees, which can grow up to 98 feet (30 m) tall. Shredded and unsweetened, the interior flesh of the ripe coconut is used extensively in South Indian cooking and in some North Indian desserts. More and more stores are beginning to carry fresh coconut, but if you cannot find it just use the prepackaged (unsweetened) shredded coconut.

- **COCONUT WATER:** When you shake a coconut, you'll hear liquid inside. This is coconut water, which is often sipped right from the large, young fruit through straws on the streets of India.

- **COCONUT MILK:** It's not the liquid in the coconut; instead, it's obtained by coarsely grating the white coconut flesh and squeezing out the liquid. One effective way to get coconut milk is to pass hot water through grated coconut held in muslin or cheesecloth or squeezed in your hands; this process will extract the oils and aromatic compounds. Coconut milk is easily stored and used to make a variety of curries. It can be found in most stores. I use light coconut milk, which has less fat.

- **CRUMBLES:** Perfect for my Spiced Crumbles with Peas (see recipe on page 205), many types of crumbles on the market mimic minced meat quite well. Brands include Quorn, Boca, and Morningstar. Some are made of soy products and some from mushrooms. They are delicious when prepped correctly. Just be sure to read the package carefully. I've been finding more and more soy-based processed foods that contain egg whites.

- **ENO:** A white fruit salt, this ingredient can act as an antacid and is added to steamed rice and lentil squares (*dhokla)* to make them light and airy. I've only seen it in a white powdery form at Indian grocery stores. If you don't have it, just substitute baking soda.

- **FLOUR (ATTA):** There are countless types of flour available, and many of them are used in Indian cooking. The most important is *chapati* flour, a finely milled whole-wheat flour used to make traditional *roti* (also called *chapati* or *phulka*), an unleavened flat bread. This flour is traditionally whole wheat, but in recent years, food distributors have begun adding the more processed, less healthy white flour called *maitha*. When you purchase this flour, make sure its label reads "100 percent whole wheat." Also, be aware that *chapati* flour is different from the whole-wheat flour found in regular grocery stores. If you try making *rotis* with regular whole-wheat flour, they'll be heavier, darker, and a little bitter. If you don't have an Indian grocery close by, look for whole-wheat pastry flour made from whole white wheat. You can also substitute a mixture of one part whole-wheat flour and one part all-purpose flour. High-protein gram flour (*besan*) is made from skinned, split, and ground black chickpeas. It is a vegan's dream, because added to many savory items (like my Tofu Chickpea Fritters [see recipe on page 103]), it acts as a binding agent and makes eggs completely unnecessary. It's also delicious blended with water and made into a quick savory pancake for breakfast. More mainstream markets are carrying "chickpea flour," but it's not clear whether this flour is made from white or black chickpeas. I've used this flour, and it works. But to avoid confusion, when I refer to gram flour I mean the traditional gram flour found at Indian grocery stores. Other breads that Indians eat include *parantha* (whole-wheat stuffed flatbread made on the stovetop like *roti*), *poori* (fried bread made from *atta*), and *makhi ki roti* (flatbread made from cornmeal). *Naan* is eaten sparingly. In this book, I have tackled *roti* and *parantha* to give you a sense of what we Indians truly eat.

- **GARLIC (LASSAN):** Garlic, like ginger and turmeric, is essential in my home—it's downright powerful. Obviously, it's a key ingredient in Indian cooking, but it's also an amazing healer. If you have a cold, fever, or sore throat, mince one clove and swallow it with a glass of water (no chewing required). You'll feel better instantly. Garlic is the first thing my daughters ask for when they get sick. Just make sure you take it after eating a little something, as it can unsettle an empty stomach. If I'm using a large amount, I often purchase it already peeled—just make sure it's fresh and that you use it up quickly.

- **GINGER ROOT (ADARAK):** Ginger, a key element in most Indian cooking, is a root that grows underground. The best ginger root, which is hard to find, is young with pinkish skin. The thinner the skin, the fresher it is. Avoid ginger root that looks old, dark, or shriveled. Once you grate or cut into it, the threads will be thick and chewy, and it won't work well in your dishes. Though my mom used chopped ginger root, I tend to grate it so it adds flavor but doesn't have a texture. For a great sore throat healer, grate a 2-inch piece of peeled ginger root and squeeze as much juice out as you can with your hand. Add lemon juice and honey. Drink up and see that sore throat disappear. My kids beg for it!

- **JAGGERY (GUR):** I still remember the day back in the 1970s when my father discovered his precious *gur* in an Indian grocery store. He was overjoyed and felt like he'd found a piece of the country he'd left behind. *Gur* is one of the purest forms of sugar, made from sugarcane stalks that are first pressed to extract all their juice. This juice is then boiled until it becomes brown, murky, and sticky; at that point, it's poured into molds to cool and solidify. The first time I saw *gur* being made was in our village, Bhikhi. The sharp smell was overpowering. Dried, discarded sugarcane husks were scattered everywhere, and the workers boiled all the good stuff. I use this as my sweetener of choice, but of course, you can use whichever sweetener you're most comfortable with.

- **MINT (*PUDINA, PODINA*):** Grown in the back yards of many Indian families, fresh mint is a key element of the North Indian dinner table. The mint used for Indian chutneys and marinades has a darker, more jagged leaf than other varieties.

- **NONDAIRY MILK:** For the few recipes that traditionally require milk, like *Adarak ki Sabji* (see recipe on page 156) and *Mattu Massi's* Cold Coffee (see recipe on page 230), soy, almond, hemp, rice, and oat milks are appropriate alternatives.

- **NUTRITIONAL YEAST:** These golden flakes, available in the bulk section of specialty grocery stores or packaged in cans, can be added to just about any meal to inject an assortment of B vitamins (including B12) and protein. I sprinkle them over my soups and mix them into my lentil dishes. They have an almost cheese-like taste and texture.

- **OIL:** The first question I'm always asked when I do cooking demos is which oil I like to use when cooking. Most people associate *ghee* (clarified butter) with Indian cuisine. I happen to have grown up in a home where *ghee* was rarely used. (Obviously, it's not part of a vegan diet.) Although some Indian cooks believe olive oil imparts a strong taste to Indian dishes, my mother never thought this was the case—especially when we used less-expensive refined olive oils, such as virgin olive oil and olive oil blends. Now that studies show heating olive oil at high heats (beyond 200 to 250°F [93 to 120°C]) can be unhealthy, I reserve it for drizzling on salads and into salad dressings and for making hummus. For cooking, I instead reach for oils that can better take the heat needed to make good Indian food, including coconut oil, grapeseed oil (which has a smoke point of up to 421°F [216°C]), and safflower oil. I really like grapeseed because of its light flavor and taste—it works particularly well with Indian foods. I like to use coconut oil for South Indian cooking. You'll be fine with any light vegetable oil or canola oil. I use flaxseed oil to moisten *roti* and *naan*, but you should never cook with flaxseed oil, as it cannot take heat. In parts of India, mustard, untoasted sesame, and peanut oils are commonly used, but these all have strong smells and tastes. Experiment with any and all. My recipes don't specify which oil you should use, because I leave it open to your taste buds and your good judgment.

- **ONIONS (*PYAZ*):** Indians love their onions—cooked and raw, sprinkled with lemon juice and spices like black salt (*kala namak*) and red chile powder. It's a good thing. This smelly vegetable is actually rich in a powerful antioxidant called quercetin, which may reduce the risk of cancer.

The crunch of raw onion is the perfect accompaniment to an Indian meal, and onion is delicious cooked with cumin, ginger root, and garlic. If the taste of raw onions is too sharp for you, slice them and soak them in water for 15 minutes. Drain the water and dry the onions before using them. The best onions for Indian cuisine are yellow and red. The white, sweet onions tend to be too sweet for our cuisine.

- **PICKLE, INDIAN (*ACHAAR*):** We Indians love our pickles, but not the ones that are more common in the West. Indian "pickles" aren't just cucumbers—they're made from anything from green chiles to mangoes, lemons, and even fresh ginger root. The fruits and vegetables are preserved in vinegar, brine, or their own juices. The taste can be sweet, spicy, sour, or a combination.

Indian pickles are used as a condiment to a main dish—to dip your bread into or to layer into your rice and lentils. For all of our road trips growing up, my mother would bring along a stack of Indian spiced bread (*paranthas*) and garnish it simply with *achaar*.

- **QUINOA:** Quinoa (pronounced KEEN-wah) is an edible seed that is often mistaken for a grain. Closely related to plant species like beets and spinach, quinoa is very high in protein and provides all nine essential amino acids, making it a complete protein. Gluten and cholesterol free, this tiny seed is a dietary must, especially for vegans or vegetarians. It cooks up easily, like rice (just follow the instructions on the package), and from there it can be substituted for rice or other grains in any recipe in this book. My Lemon Brown Rice (see recipe on page 194) made with quinoa was a bigger hit than the original rice dish. When I make rice, I often substitute ½ cup rice (87 g) with ½ cup quinoa (85 g) to make a mixed pilaf. I also include it in soups and sprinkle it cooked over salads.

- **RICE (CHAWAL):** Basmati, one of the most coveted varieties of rice in the world, means "fragrant" in Sanskrit. Its grains are thin and slender, and it tastes delicious when paired with Indian curries. I've actually visited a rice mill in Punjab and stood under the rice as it poured into a giant pile from an overhead chute. As more and more people today opt for the nutritional benefits of brown rice, you can now find many brown basmati options that taste and cook better than the varieties offered in years past. Though I love the taste of white basmati rice, I use brown basmati as my everyday go-to and keep the white on hand for an occasional treat.

- **SEITAN:** Chewy and dense, this meat-free ingredient mimics meat. It is made from wheat gluten and can be used in various curries and soups, such as my Seitan Mulligatawny Soup (see recipe on page 88). If you follow a gluten-free diet, you should be careful to avoid seitan, but today some seitan brands are made without gluten. Ask around and read packaging carefully.

- **TAMARIND (IMLEE, IMLI):** Key to South Indian cooking, tamarind is the pulp collected from the long, brown pods that hang from tamarind trees. These pods are used to make the souring agent used in *Rasam* Powder (see recipe on page 61), Tamarind Brown Rice (see recipe on page 196), and Stovetop *Sambhar*-Inspired Curry (see recipe on page 144). The best way to use this ingredient is to make the juice yourself by soaking the pulp in hot water and then straining it. Tamarind paste is also available in Indian grocery stores, but it tends to be a lot stronger and sharper, so you should add it to your dishes in small amounts until you get the balance just right.

- **TEMPEH:** This ingredient is actually fermented soybean cake. It can be used in place of tofu and seitan in recipes, including in my Tofu Curry (see recipe on page 210). It is dense and thick, with a nutty flavor. I've seen tempeh sautéed, chopped, and seared. It's delicious and worth trying.

- **TOFU:** Basic tofu is made from soybeans, water, and a curdling agent. It absorbs flavors well and is high in protein and calcium and low in fat and calories. Having lived in Hawaii and Japan, I've never been afraid of tofu. Like anything else, including meat, tofu is very bland if not prepared correctly and brimming with flavor when it is. For Indian food, I prefer to use extra-firm organic tofu. Just about every brand of tofu products offers this option these days. Japanese silken tofu comes in a box and is often stored in the nonrefrigerated international aisle of a grocery store. When blended, this super-soft tofu can be mixed with almost any ingredient to mimic dairy-style binding agents. It is often used to make desserts, such as vegan cheesecake. In this book, I use it for my *Tukri Pakora* appetizer (see recipe on page 104).

- **TOMATOES:** When preparing Italian dishes, you're told to look for the darkest and sweetest tomatoes available. For Indian food, you need to go in the opposite direction. The key is to use tomatoes with just the right amount of tart to offset the spices in your dish. I love plum tomatoes, which are just the right size and taste for Indian cooking. In many of my dishes I call for peeled tomatoes, which are easy to prepare. The traditional method is to cut an X into the nonstem end of each tomato with a sharp knife and add the tomatoes to boiling water. Cook for 1 to 2 minutes, until the peel starts to pull off. Pull the tomatoes out of the water using tongs, let them cool, and then peel them. The absolute fastest way to do this is with a serrated peeler (my new go-to kitchen gadget).

- **SUGAR OR SWEETENER:** Whenever a recipe calls for sweetener, I've used jaggery (*gur*), brown sugar, agave nectar (a low-glycemic sweetener most often made from the blue agave plant), or Sucanat (pure dried sugar cane juice).

- **VEGAN MAYONNAISE:** The two brands I use the most are Nayonaise and Vegenaise. Either will work perfectly in my Mock Egg Salad (see recipe on page 206).

- **YOGURT:** The one reason it's been so difficult for me to go completely vegan is my cultural tie to and love of yogurt—especially homemade Indian yogurt, which is a little thinner and more tart than its supermarket equivalent. Also, in the past, soy yogurt available on grocery store shelves has always been sweetened and flavored with fruit. Unsweetened, plain soy yogurt has started to appear at specialty stores, including Whole Foods Market. It's not exactly the same flavor, but it's pretty darn good. I use Whole Soy & Co. The absolute key is to read the label carefully: the yogurt must be unsweetened, and not just plain, in order to work in Indian recipes.

Tools of the Trade

With just a few basic tools at your fingertips, you'll be making delicious Indian food in no time. Most likely, you already have most of the basics: a variety of knives, cutting boards, whisks, tongs, and measuring spoons. A few other key items and a basic knowledge of cooking terms will help round out your Indian kitchen.

Dum is the process of cooking food in its own steam. Traditionally, this was done in large pots that were sealed with dough so that no steam was released during cooking. Whenever a recipe instructs you to turn down the heat, put the lid on the container, and let the dish cook, it's telling you to follow the rules of *dum* cooking. The slow cooker is a modern-day take on this style of cooking.

The traditional way to cook Indian food is to season it with a *tarka*, which is also called a *chounk* or *vaghar*. This simply means that after cooking a lentil dish (*dal*) or before cooking a dry dish (such as Crackling Okra [see recipe on page 178]), you heat your oil and add the spices needed for the dish. Once the cumin, mustard seeds, or other spices start to sizzle, brown, and change color, the oil is ready to be added to your food. The slow cooker has allowed me to eliminate this step from many recipes because the spices actually break down over the longer cooking times. Some slow cooker users still make a *tarka* on the side. *Bhuna* means to roast spices or other ingredients dry or in oil. This process creates texture and taste. *Rasa* is essentially the broth that is created for many dishes, including homemade cheese with peas (*mattar paneer*). The word also refers to the process of cooking spices together with, say, ginger root, garlic, and tomatoes to create a broth—essentially a curry sauce. This sauce is thinned out with water, boiled, and then allowed to simmer for some time, until it is thick and flavorful.

- **BLENDER OR FOOD PROCESSOR:** It's essential to have a strong, heavy-duty blender. For the last five years I've used a powerful Vitamix blender, which is one of best machines on the market. It's strong enough to pulverize cantaloupe seeds, make ice cream, and make green juice without eliminating the fiber. Granted, these machines are expensive, but if you go this route you won't regret it. Another handy tool for blending is an immersion blender. This relatively inexpensive hand-held blender can be used to easily break down curries and soups right in the cooking vessel. It's also great to have a food processor handy to quickly grind down ginger root, garlic, and onions for basic *masalas*.

- **DOUBLE BOILER:** This is essentially a cooking vessel with two compartments that allows you to boil water on the bottom to cook items in the top container. Typically, it's used to melt chocolate. I use my double boiler to steam *dhokla*.

- **KETTLE:** If you need to add water to dishes as they cook, it's best to add boiling water so you don't lose precious cooking time. I rely on my electric kettle to boil water quickly and easily. It's also great to have on hand when you need to add water to a slow cooker, as cold or lukewarm water would interrupt the cooking cycle.

- **MEAT TENDERIZER OR POUNDER:** Blasphemy to add this item to a vegan cookbook? Not really, if it's used in the right way. This is the best tool I've found to peel garlic—even better than a large chef's knife. I realized this when I was testing my *Adarak Masala* (see recipe on page 64), which calls for one hundred cloves of garlic (!). Of course, my husband couldn't find the prepeeled variety. I sighed, pulled out the meat tenderizer, and banged down once on each clove. The skins fell away easily, and I got all my aggressions out at the same time!

- **MICROPLANE GRATER:** I own the most useful Microplane grater on the planet, but I can't seem to remember where I purchased it or find an exact replica anywhere. The ones on the market now have very tiny holes (better for grating dry spices) or are big and difficult to clean. The one I have is tiny enough to stick in your back pocket, but with medium-sized holes— essential when grating ginger root or garlic. I take it with me to all my cooking demos, and everyone who's tried to steal it so far has been unsuccessful!

- **POTS AND PANS:** I've used the same pots and pans since I received them as wedding gifts in 1999. Yours don't have to be high-tech either. But for Indian cooking, they should be thick and heavy. Indian curries turn out best when they're cooked over low flame in a heavy pot or pan. I use a flat griddle to make Indian flatbreads such as *roti* or *parantha*. A *tava* is the traditional Indian iron griddle, but any good quality, flat, heavy pan will do. An Indian *karahi* (pronounced ka-ra-hee) is essentially a wok and is used for deep frying. I have not included any deep-fried dishes in this book, but it's useful to know that this type of pan is used for frying up Indian breads like *pooris* and making fried snacks like *samosas*.

- **ROLLING PIN:** Have one handy for rolling out traditional Indian flatbreads such as *rotis* and *paranthas*. I also use my rolling pin to loosen pomegranate seeds and to grind roasted cumin seeds when I don't feel like pulling out my spice grinder.

- **SERRATED PEELER:** Tammy Brawley, the culinary director of a Sur La Table store in Richmond, Virginia, demonstrated this amazing device to me. I was teaching a class and needed to peel a tomato. I was about to boil water and do it the traditional way, when she pulled out a serrated peeler. The jagged edges on the peeler make taking the skin off tomatoes and peaches a piece of cake. It's the best and cheapest kitchen contraption you'll ever find.

- **SIFTER:** This is great to have around to sift flour and homemade spice blends.

- **SLOW COOKER:** Ever since I wrote my first cookbook, *The Indian Slow Cooker*, I've been bombarded with questions about the best slow cooker. It's hard to make generalizations about models because after two years of research, I've found that there is no real gold standard when it comes to these devices. One model can differ greatly from another and differ still more from a third. The key when purchasing one is that it should have several beneficial functions: a removable inner cooking insert to make cleaning easy, different cooking settings (low, high, and warm), and a timer. I always recommend having at least two sizes, depending on your cooking needs. I love the 3½-quart (3.32-L) size (I use the Cuisinart) to cook for your family on a day-to-day basis. My 5-quart (4.74-L) Rival comes in handy for cooking larger quantities and for parties. I have a 6-quart All Clad slow cooker that I just love. It was expensive, and since it holds 6½ quarts (6.16 L), it's useful for parties. There are smaller slow cookers that can work for Indian cooking if they have different heat settings. Beans do not cook well in a slow cooker that doesn't have a "high" setting. Slow cookers are safe and use much less electricity than a conventional gas or electric oven. On the low setting, they use the same amount of electricity as a 75-watt light bulb, and on the high setting they still use less than a 300-watt bulb. They can be left on safely while you are out of the house; just clear the area around the slow cooker and the cord. Another rule of thumb is to make sure your slow cooker is filled at least halfway and that you don't overfill it. Once a dish starts to cook, it expands. If you're not sure whether your slow cooker will be overfilled or not, just decrease the amount of water you use by a cup or two, and then add boiled water halfway through the cooking process. If you don't have a slow cooker, don't worry. You can make any slow cooker dish in a heavy pot, such as a Dutch oven. Just reduce the amount of water used by ½ to 1 cup and use a very low flame. You'll have to experiment with exact water and cooking times, and of course, you'll have to stay home to tend to the stove.

- **SPICE BOX (*MASALA DABBA*):** Every Indian home cook I know has at least one. This traditionally round, stainless steel box comes with seven round bowls that hold individual spices. The box can be kept on your counter or in a drawer to be pulled out for cooking. It's an easy way to dole out your spices without fussing with lids and grabbing for jars in the back of your cabinet. I have my own version, which can be purchased on my website, www.indianASapplepie.com, or at Williams-Sonoma (www.williams-sonoma.com). Mine allows you to level your spices right in your small containers and comes with a measuring teaspoon and tablespoon that fit right into your box. I have eight of these boxes for each grouping of spices I use, including Mexican, East Asian, Greek, and soup. I have one box that sits on the dining table for dinner spices like salt and ground pepper and another for oatmeal toppings. The possibilities are endless.

- **SPICE GRINDER:** Grinding your own spices is much easier than you think if you have the right tools. The best and most basic way to grind spices and spice blends quickly is to purchase a simple coffee grinder and use it only for spices. If you don't mind using a little muscle, you can use a mortar and pestle. If you have a powerful blender, such as a Vitamix, use its smaller dry jug to grind your spice blends. I've been using this option more frequently to grind larger batches of blends. The key is to break up your cassia leaves, whole dried red chile peppers, and cinnamon sticks before grinding so they grind down completely.

Legumes: Lentils, Beans, and Peas

Low in fat. No cholesterol. High in folate, potassium, iron, and magnesium. Extremely high in soluble and insoluble fiber. Super high in protein. Incredibly cheap. The world's perfect food? You decide.

It's no wonder that the most recent medical research has shown that legumes (which are also called pulses) are superfoods. Although the West just now seems to be catching on, Indians have been privy to this valuable information for centuries. It's just not necessary to eat meat to get sufficient protein as long as you combine your legumes with grains. Both categories are deficient in different amino acids, but you can make up for the individual deficiency by combining them—not even on the same plate, but in a general, well-rounded diet. So if you had oatmeal in the morning, the beans you eat in your salad later in the day will balance out your protein intake for the day.

Now that the West has started to overcome this nutritional learning curve, it's time to learn how to cook this amazing category of food. I've been on a mission the last few years to teach people what legumes are and what to do with them.

I conduct food tours in Chicago and around the country. The one grocery aisle that seems to baffle everyone is the one where beans and lentils are stocked. There are bags upon bags of different colors and sizes, from green, to red, to black, and even orange. Where does one even start? The best way is to first take a deep breath. Everything you are looking at is from the same food category: legumes.

Simply put, legumes are seeds that grow in a pod. Everything you see in bags on a grocery shelf is a dried version of these fresh seeds. Take a chickpea, for example. In India, vendors sell fresh chickpea stalks door to door from carts. The chickpeas are young and green and still in the pods. My girls love to take the pods, open them up like peanut shells, and gobble up the raw, green chickpeas inside. Dry out these green, wrinkled seeds, and you've essentially got the dried chickpeas you buy from the store. Rarely is the fresh version of any of these legumes seen in the United States (unless you find them in an Indian grocery store), and that's why I believe it's harder in the West to connect the dots.

Legumes include lentils, beans, and peas. Believe it or not, peanuts are technically legumes and not nuts. This is why someone with an allergy to peanuts may also be allergic to other seeds grown in pods—lentils, beans, and peas.

Now, just because there seem to be hundreds of different-looking bags on the shelves does not mean there are hundreds of varieties out there. Every whole legume is offered (in most cases) in four stages:

- The whole form of any legume with the skin intact. On the package label, the Hindi word *sabud* or *sabut* before the type of legume will indicate that it is in its original form, with nothing removed. This is the most wholesome form, but it also requires more water and time to cook.
- The whole legume without the skin.
- The split legume with the skin on (called *chilka*, which means "skin" in Hindi).
- The split legume without the skin (called *dhuli*, which means "washed" in Hindi).

Try cooking these different forms of the same lentil and/or bean, and you'll have surprisingly different results—in taste and in texture. In India, many of these soupy preparations are called *dal*. In our Punjabi household, we only referred to soupy lentils as *dal*. In other parts of India, dry legume dishes are also referred to as *dal*. I know it can get confusing, but it's all delicious if you keep just a few pointers in mind.

- **CLEANING YOUR LEGUMES WELL.** Depending on where you purchase your beans and lentils, you may find debris and small rocks mixed in. This is especially true for products from Indian grocery stores, and especially for black lentils, which mix in seamlessly with small pieces of dark stones. The best way to clean them is to put about a cup of the product on the edge of a white plate farthest away from you. Slowly bring small amounts of the product toward you, picking out any foreign matter along the way. Enlist your kids for this task. Mine will drop everything to come and clean beans and lentils—go figure!
- **STORING YOUR LEGUMES WITHOUT WASHING.** Never, ever store beans or lentils damp or wet. They can easily become moldy and spoil. Store them dry in a dark, cool place, ideally in glass containers, and they will last for up to six months.
- **DISCARDING SPOILED LEGUMES.** It doesn't happen often, but you can get a bad batch of legumes. Because you are working with very fresh and perishable whole foods, insects can contaminate them. This has happened to me only once, but you'll notice that the beans or lentils at the bottom of your container will look eaten away and powdered. If you notice anything like this, let the shop where you purchased them know immediately, and get rid of them.
- **SOAKING OR NOT SOAKING?** This is the million-dollar question. Many say that beans that have been soaked eliminate gas later. I've never noticed any difference—maybe because we are so used to eating them. (Ironically, I find that the bloating and gas come more from meat and dairy.) Because my life with two little kids is so hectic, if I take the time to soak the beans I'll

never get around to cooking them. Soak if you feel better doing so. If you do soak them over-night, just pull back on the water levels in the recipe by a cup or two and decrease the cooking time by one or two hours. You'll have to play with it a bit to get it perfect. Kidney beans are the exception. According to some theories, you're better off soaking them for a few hours, rinsing them, and then using them.

- **STORING COOKED LEGUMES.** Most legumes, once cooked, will keep from three days to one week in the refrigerator and up to three months in the freezer. The beauty of cooking beans and lentils is that they freeze incredibly well.

- **REHEATING LEGUMES.** You can reheat beans and lentils in the microwave. I prefer the stove. As they sit in the refrigerator or freezer, they soak up more liquid and will seem to dry out a bit. Just add a little water and heat them slowly, on a low flame. If you add more water, add a little salt to compensate for the lost flavor.

- **USING CANNED VARIETIES.** This is a definite time saver. I do use canned chickpeas and black beans on occasion, but I don't like the added salt or additives, nor do I like how mushy the product becomes. If you use canned, rinse them well to remove any additives.

There are many varieties of legumes out there. Here, I've included my favorites and others used for the recipes in this book.

- **ADZUKI OR AZUKI BEANS (RED CHORI):** These beans are tiny, red, and used largely in Japanese desserts. My years spent studying Japanese cooking in Japan and in Hawaii meant I just had to experiment with this delicious and addictive little bean. It holds up incredibly well in the slow cooker and gives my Brown Rice and Adzuki Bean *Dhokla* (see recipe on page 122) a nice twist.

- **BLACK BEANS:** These are not common at all in Indian cooking, but I'm not sure why. I made a *kitchari* with them and was blown away by how delicious the results were. Even if you are making Mexican food, use my cooking times in this book for Cooked, Plain Black Beans (see recipe on page 129), and you won't be tied to the stove for hours waiting for them to cook.

- **BLACK LENTILS, BLACK GRAM (URAD, MAA, MATPE BEANS):** This is one of the most widely-used lentils in North Indian cooking and Hindu religious ceremonies. It's what you think of when you order a *dal makhani* dish at an Indian restaurant. They are very easy to recognize because they are jet black, tiny, and oval-shaped. Like other lentils, they come in four forms: whole with the skin on (*sabut urad*), whole without the skin, split with the skin (*urad dal*), and split without the skin.

- **BROWN LENTILS (MASOOR, MASAR, MUSSOOR):** Since my last book, these have become my go-to lentils. They hold up incredibly well cooked plain in a slow cooker and then used throughout the week for salads and quick curries. My daughter Neha says this is her favorite lunchbox item. These lentils are small, round, and dark brown. In the West, they are more easily recognized split and skinned—uncooked, they have an almost salmon color, and they are referred to as red lentils or *masoor dal*. It's a bit bizarre, but when they're cooked, they turn yellow (sort of like saffron!). The split and skinned version of this lentil cooks quickly and makes a very easy meal when you are short on time.

- **CHICKPEAS (CHANA):** The chickpeas available in the West are the large, white variety. In India, we have two varieties. The large, white type is known as *kabuli chana*. Most know what *kabuli chana* is, but often buy it canned. I double dare you to try it the way I suggest cooking it in this book—from dried. You will absolutely love the texture and firmness. The second type of chickpea is known as *kala chana*. This smaller, tougher variety is available in black and green. There's no difference in taste. It is absolutely delicious and, according to my father, so high in protein that they fed it to the horses in his village when he was little. These tiny chickpeas are easy to sprout. They are also split, dried, and ground down to make *besan*—chickpea flour.

- **SPLIT GRAM (CHANA DAL):** *Chana dal* is the split and skinned version of the black chickpea. It looks like and is often confused with split peas and the split version of *toor dal*, so label containers well. This split lentil or bean is used often in South Indian dishes and spice blends.

- **COWPEAS, BLACK-EYED PEAS OR BEANS (*LOBHIA, RONGI*), AND RED COW-PEAS (*SABUT CHOWLI*):** Since my first book, my kids and I have become huge fans of black-eyed peas. They have so much flavor without any seasoning—not to mention what they taste like when they are seasoned. They hold up really well throughout the day, so they are a favorite for the kids' lunchboxes. Try them Goan style, with some coconut milk, or as a basic North Indian curry. I even have a recipe for Indian-style hummus that works well for these delicious beans.
- **GREEN LENTILS, GREEN GRAM (*MOONG, MUNG*):** Probably one of the more commonly known lentils in the West, these small green counterparts to the black lentil are easy to find and just as easy to cook. The split and skinned version (yellow *mung*) is one of the fastest-cooking lentils on the planet. I can whip it up for my kids in 20 minutes flat.
- **KIDNEY BEANS (*RAJMAH*):** My girls were on their annual visit to their pediatrician, Daphne Hirsch, when she asked them their favorite food. They both blurted out, "*Rajmah!*" It's a Punjabi comfort food, as no other region in India cooks kidney beans to perfection like we do. Every household has its own tweaks, but there is nothing like kidney beans made Indian style.
- **LIMA BEANS (*PAVTA*):** A large, flat bean similar to the kidney bean, lima beans are at once light and hearty, and they are delicious in Indian curries. I substituted them for kidney beans in one of my slow cooker dishes to rave reviews.
- **PIGEON PEAS (*TOOR DAL, TOOVAR, ARHAR, AND TUR*):** This lentil is used quite a bit in West and South India. The split and skinned version is used in making *sambhar* and *rasam*. It is sold split, skinned, and dry, or with an oily film on it. I recommend that you avoid the oily version. They're harder to wash.
- **YELLOW SPLIT PEAS:** These are the dried yellow version of the green pea. They are wonderful when cooked in a slow cooker and blended into a soup (as in my last book). In this book, I didn't include any recipes that call for split peas, but feel free to substitute them in recipes that call for other lentils. I'm going to save my experimenting with this one for future books.

KABULI CHANA

KALA CHANA

MASOOR DAL / RED SPLIT LENTIL

RAJMAH

SABAT URAD / BLACK LENTIL

MOONG DAL, SPLIT AND SKINNED

TOOR DAL

SPLIT TOOR

URAD DAL, SPLIT AND SKINNED

Spice Blends and Other Shortcuts

Most traditional households in India blend their own spices. This seemingly complicated process is actually very easy. Homemade spice blends are fresh, delicious, and—best of all—salt and additive free. Most of the blends below are recipes made by my grandmother in Chandigarh, India. Some were developed by friends from other regions in India. And still others resulted from extensive research and testing.

Know that no recipe has to be followed exactly. If you don't have ground ginger on hand, for example, just omit it. If you don't like the taste of coriander, increase the cumin or other spices. If you have a lower tolerance for heat, pull back on the chile peppers. Make these your own blends.

Grind the blends in a coffee grinder reserved for spices or in the dry jug of a powerful blender, such as a Vitamix. Getting them finely ground is important (so they don't taste gritty later), so prepare to be patient, grind in batches, and sift the blends before storing to get rid of any bits of cinnamon sticks or other spices that don't break down completely. Once they are ground, store your blends in airtight containers in a cool, dark place for up to six months. Whole spices will keep for years. But once you grind them and release their essential oils, they become perishable. Of course, there are always exceptions, and if you have a ground spice lying around longer that still smells aromatic, go ahead and use it up. I just wouldn't keep ground spices for much longer than six months.

If you are in a pinch, of course, purchase a box of any of the blends below from your local Indian grocery store, remembering to carefully read the ingredient list. Many commercial blends lately have started to add salt, which can greatly alter the taste and balance of your finished dish.

Note: Some of these recipes combine whole with ground spices. Whenever you are required to roast a blend, make sure you roast the whole spices first and add in the powders when you grind them. If you heat the powders with the whole spices, the powder will burn before you get the whole spices roasted. How do I know this? I made this very mistake when conducting a spice-grinding workshop with a dozen pairs of eyes following my every move. It's also very helpful to first break up cinnamon sticks, cassia or bay leaves, and whole red chiles before processing them in a grinder.

Chai (Tea) Masala

YIELD: ¾ CUP (178 ML)

I grew up with a mortar and pestle always within reach, so I could grind a few spices just so for a quick cup of chai *for my parents. This blend is my own personal combination—ingredients that are traditional in* chai *but also include a few healing spices that I always use when making* chai *for my kids—such as black cardamom and turmeric to help ward off coughs and colds.*

1 tablespoon whole black peppercorns

9 (3-inch [7.5-cm]) cinnamon sticks, broken into pieces

1 tablespoon whole cloves

½ teaspoon fennel seeds

2 tablespoons whole green cardamom pods

3 black cardamom pods

2 tablespoons ground ginger

1 teaspoon turmeric powder

1. Put all the ingredients in a spice grinder or in the dry jug of a powerful blender, such as a Vitamix. Process to a fine powder. Sift after grinding to get a finer powder. Store in an airtight container in a cool, dry place for up to 6 months.

Note: To make traditional *chai*, add 1 teaspoon of this mix to 4 cups (948 mL) boiling water. Add 2 black tea bags, ½ cup (119 mL) soy milk (or alternative), and honey or agave nectar to taste. Boil for a few minutes, remove the tea bags, and serve immediately piping hot. For a richer flavor, add a teaspoon of freshly grated ginger root. This spice mix may be also be sprinkled over baked potatoes, used in spiced nuts, and even added to your holiday eggnog or apple pie.

Chaat Masala

YIELD: 2 CUPS (474 ML)

The word chaat *holds a ton of meaning for me. It refers to the idea of licking your fingers clean because the food was so good. That's how I felt the first time I can remember encountering* chaat masala *on the streets of India. I was twelve, visiting the sacred temples in the hills of Vaishno Devi with my family. Outside one of the shrines, I encountered a white, juicy daikon skinned and split, served on a little metal tray. It dripped with fresh lime juice and was doused with red chile powder that seared my lips before ever touching them. And there was the* chaat masala—*likely roasted and ground to the specifics of that street vendor's home. Ever since, I've been addicted to fresh veggies and the utter simplicity of that moment and memory. This* masala *is used mostly on fresh ingredients and street foods. Try it on raw veggies, sprinkle it over boiled potatoes, or stir a pinch into your plain soy yogurt.*

½ heaping cup (40 g) coriander seeds

2 heaping tablespoons cumin seeds

2 heaping tablespoons fennel seeds

8 whole dried red chiles, broken into pieces

½ cup (50 g) whole black peppercorns

2 heaping teaspoons mango powder (*amchur*)

2 tablespoons black salt (*kala namak*)

2 heaping teaspoons ground ginger

2 heaping teaspoons carom seeds (*ajwain*)

1. In a shallow, heavy pan, dry roast the coriander, cumin, fennel, and red chiles over medium heat. Stay close, and shake the pan every 15 to 20 seconds to prevent the spices from burning. They should be just toasted and aromatic. After about 4 minutes of roasting, transfer the mixture to a plate and allow it to cool for 15 minutes.

2. Once the mixture is cool, transfer it to a spice grinder or the dry jug of a powerful blender, such as a Vitamix. Add the remaining ingredients and process to a fine powder. You may need to grind it—do so in small batches, depending on the size of your grinder. Sift after grinding to get a finer powder. Store in an airtight container for up to 6 months.

Chana (Chole, Chholay) Masala

YIELD: 1½ CUPS (356 ML)

This is the perfect spice blend for the spicy chickpea curry called chana masala. *(It's a little confusing, but the dish and the spice blend go by the same name.) The key to this spice blend is the dried pomegranate seeds, which lend a needed sourness to the dish. Sheer perfection!*

¼ cup (24 g) cumin seeds

¼ cup (20 g) coriander seeds

¼ cup (28 g) dried pomegranate seeds (*anardana*)

2 teaspoons black mustard seeds

2 teaspoons fenugreek seeds

10 whole cloves

2 black cardamom pods

4 green cardamom pods

3 (3-inch [7.5-cm]) cinnamon sticks, broken into pieces

1 teaspoon carom seeds (*ajwain*)

1 tablespoon whole black peppercorns

5 medium cassia leaves (or bay leaves), broken into pieces

10 whole dried red chiles, broken into pieces

1 tablespoon dried fenugreek leaves (*kasoori methi*)

2 tablespoons mango powder (*amchur*)

1 tablespoon ground ginger

1 tablespoon black salt (*kala namak*)

1. In a shallow, heavy pan, dry roast the cumin, coriander, pomegranate seeds, mustard, fenugreek seeds, cloves, black and green cardamom pods, cinnamon, carom, peppercorns, cassia or bay leaves, red chiles, and fenugreek leaves over medium heat. Stay close, and shake the pan every 15 to 20 seconds to prevent the spices from burning. They should be just toasted and aromatic. After about 4 minutes of roasting, transfer the mixture to a plate and allow it to cool for 15 minutes.

2. Once the mixture is cool, transfer it to a spice grinder or the dry jug of a powerful blender, such as a Vitamix. Add the mango powder, ginger, and black salt and process to a fine powder. You may need to grind it in small batches, depending on the size of your grinder. Sift after grinding to get a finer powder. Store in an airtight container for up to 6 months.

Mattu Massi's Garam Masala

YIELD: 2½ CUPS (593 ML)

In Hindi, garam *means "warm" or "hot," while* masala *means "blend of spices." This combination of spices has become synonymous with North Indian cooking. There's no one* garam masala *recipe—every household has its own magical blend. The recipe below is my grandmother's (Beeji's) that my Mattu Massi (maternal aunt) in Chandigarh grinds to this day. The only thing I changed is that I added coriander seeds, which Massi says she normally avoids because this tends to make the mixture spoil in warm climates. I also dry roasted the spices. You can grind them without roasting them as Massi does. Just know that roasting the spices makes them more pungent, and you should use a little less of the roasted version of* garam masala *than you would of the unroasted version.*

1 cup (96 g) cumin seeds

½ cup (40 g) coriander seeds

¼ cup (21 g) black cardamom pods

12 (3-inch [7.5-cm]) cinnamon sticks, broken into pieces

¼ cup (21 g) whole cloves

¼ cup (25 g) whole black peppercorn

2 whole nutmegs (or 1 tablespoon ground nutmeg)

1. In a shallow, heavy pan, dry roast all ingredients over medium heat. (If using ground nutmeg, wait until the next step to add it or the powder will burn.) Stay close and shake the pan every 15 to 20 seconds to prevent the spices from burning. The spices should be just toasted and aromatic. After about 4 minutes of roasting, transfer the mixture to a plate and allow it to cool for 15 minutes.

2. Once the mixture is cool, transfer the ingredients to a spice grinder or the dry jug of a powerful blender, such as a Vitamix. (Add the ground nutmeg at this point, if using.) Process to a fine powder. You may need to process it in small batches, depending on the size of your grinder. Sift after grinding to get a finer powder. Store in an airtight container for up to 6 months.

Sambhar Masala

YIELD: 1 CUP (237 ML)

This is the key spice in the dish sambhar, a South Indian lentil and vegetable stew most commonly eaten with dosas. But don't limit yourself. I love this spice blend so much that I often add it to other lentil and bean dishes or sprinkle it over rice and even homemade popcorn.

¼ cup (48 g) split gram (*chana dal*)

1 tablespoon split and skinned black lentils (*dhuli urad*)

1 tablespoon split and skinned green lentils (*dhuli moong*)

½ cup (40 g) coriander seeds

½ cup (42 g) whole dried red chiles, broken into pieces

½ cup (11 g) firmly packed fresh curry leaves, roughly chopped

1 heaping tablespoon cumin seeds

1 heaping tablespoon black mustard seeds

1 heaping tablespoon white poppy seeds

1 tablespoon fenugreek seeds

2 (3-inch [7.5-cm]) cinnamon sticks, broken into pieces

20 whole black peppercorns

3 tablespoons (20 g) turmeric powder

1. In a shallow, heavy pan, dry roast all the ingredients except the turmeric over medium heat. When putting them into the pan, start with the lentils so they are closest to the heat and cook through. Shake or mix frequently, and watch closely that the mixture does not burn. (You have to especially watch the poppy seeds, which cook quickly. They can also be added toward the end of cooking.) Once the lentils brown, the curry leaves start to curl up, and the spices smell aromatic (about 7 minutes), transfer the mixture to a large plate or bowl and allow it to cool for 15 minutes.

2. Once the mixture is cool, transfer it, along with the turmeric, to a spice grinder or the dry jug of a powerful blender, such as a Vitamix. You may need to grind it in small batches, depending on the size of your grinder. Sift after grinding to get a finer powder. Store in an airtight container for up to 6 months.

Rasam Powder

YIELD: 3 CUPS (711 ML)

Many South Indian meals start with a small bowl of thin, spicy tomato soup called rasam. *This is the flavorful spice blend that is used to make the delicious and nutritious soup by the same name. You can use it for soup or use it to make a quick Indian-inspired dish.*

1 heaping tablespoon split gram (*chana dal*)

1 heaping tablespoon split and skinned pigeon peas (*toor dal*)

2 cups (160 g) coriander seeds

½ cup (48 g) cumin seeds

½ cup (50 g) whole black peppercorns

½ teaspoon fenugreek seeds

10 whole dried red chiles, broken into pieces

15 whole curry leaves, roughly chopped

1 teaspoon turmeric powder

1. In a shallow, heavy pan, dry roast all the ingredients except the turmeric over medium heat. When putting them into the pan, start with the lentils so they are closest to the heat and cook through. Shake or mix frequently, and watch closely that the mixture does not burn. Once the lentils brown, the curry leaves start to curl up, and the spices smell aromatic (about 4 minutes), transfer the mixture to a large plate or bowl and allow it to cool for 15 minutes.

2. Once the mixture is cool, add the turmeric and transfer to a spice grinder or the dry jug of a powerful blender, such as a Vitamix. You may need to grind it in small batches, depending on the size of your grinder. Sift after grinding to get a finer powder. Store in an airtight container for up to 6 months.

Roasted Ground Cumin (*Bhuna hua Jeera*)

YIELD: 1 CUP (237 ML)

Roasting and grinding your own cumin is so easy you'll never have to purchase the ground version of this spice again. I call this getting double duty from your spices—it's a way to save money and use up cumin seeds that might be tucked away in the back of your cabinet. The roasted powder is used on all sorts of savories, from yogurts (raitas) to Indian snacks called chaat. *It can also be used to put a new twist on a stew or any main dish.*

1 cup (96 g) cumin seeds

1. Heat a heavy, shallow pan over medium heat.

2. Add the cumin and roast for about 3 minutes, shaking constantly. This is essentially like dry roasting pine nuts. The key here is to never step away, to ensure the seeds don't burn.

3. Once the seeds are reddish brown, transfer them to a cold plate and let them cool for about 15 minutes. If they burn (and it's OK—I've been there many times) discard them and start again. Again, I can't emphasize enough that you need to stand right there as they roast. Three minutes goes by surprisingly fast.

4. Once they are cool, put the seeds in a spice grinder or the dry jug of a powerful blender, such as a Vitamix. You may need to grind them in small batches, depending on the size of your grinder. (No need to sift.) Store in an airtight container for up to six months.

Note: If you don't have a grinder, a Vitamix blender, or a mortar and pestle, place the roasted whole cumin between two paper towels and roll over the top sheet with a rolling pin. Press hard and continue to roll until you have a fine powder. This is best done in small batches.

North Indian Tomato Soup Stock (*Gila Masala*)

SLOW COOKER SIZE: 3½ QUART (3.32 L);
COOKING TIME: 7 HOURS TOTAL ON HIGH; YIELD: 4½ CUPS (1.1 L)

My earliest memory as a young girl is of my father sitting at our kitchen table peeling and chopping onions, tomatoes, ginger root, and garlic for my mother. One weekend a month, he would assemble cutting boards, newspapers for trash, and knives for this ritual that would take most of the day. My mother would then cook it all down into a stock to have on hand for the month. An Indian curry was easy to whip up with a few cups of gila masala on hand. My mother-in-law was the one to suggest using a slow cooker to avoid being tied to the stove all day. Now I just have to convince my husband to help with the peeling and chopping!

1 large onion, peeled and roughly chopped (3 cups [450 g])

4 large tomatoes, peeled and roughly chopped (6 cups [960 g])

1 cup (96 g) peeled and roughly chopped ginger root

10 cloves garlic, peeled and trimmed

1 tablespoon turmeric powder

¼ cup oil (59 mL)

1. Put all the ingredients into the slow cooker and mix gently. (See page 47 for details on making this dish without a slow cooker.)

2. Cook on high for 6 hours.

3. Process the mixture until smooth using an immersion blender, a traditional blender, a food processor, or a powerful blender, such as a Vitamix.

4. Return the mixture to the slow cooker and cook for another hour on high. Store in the refrigerator for up to 1 week or in the freezer for up to 3 months. You can also store it in an ice-cube tray in the freezer and pull a few cubes out when you're ready to cook a dish.

Cooking Tip: Having this stock on hand will make cooking incredibly easy. All of your basic North Indian ingredients have already been cooked and mixed. Now all you have to do is add your veggies, lentils or beans, spices, and salt. The possible uses are endless, but the most basic is: In a deep, heavy pan, heat 1 tablespoon oil over medium-high heat. Add 1 teaspoon cumin or mustard seeds. Once they sizzle, add 1 cup (237 mL) *gila masala*; 4 tablespoons (59 mL) Cashew Cream (optional; see recipe on page 65); ½ to 1 cup (119 to 237 mL) water; and any main ingredient, such as 2 cups (300 g) chopped vegetables (cauliflower/green beans/eggplant/potatoes), 2 cups (396 g) cooked beans/lentils, 14 ounces (397 g) baked and cubed tofu with 1 cup (145 g) peas, 14 ounces (397 g) cubed seitan or tempeh, or a combination. Add 1 teaspoon each *garam masala*, ground coriander, coarse sea salt, and red chile powder or cayenne. Bring the mixture to a boil, reduce the heat to medium-low, and simmer for 12 to 15 minutes, until the vegetables soften. Garnish with chopped green chiles and fresh cilantro. Here, you are only limited by your imagination. Try any combination you can drum up.

To make this dish in a 5-quart (4.74-L) slow cooker, double all the ingredients except the tomatoes (I use 8 cups [1.3 kg] to make it more tomato heavy) and cook on high for 10 hours. Blend, and cook on high for another hour. Makes 8 cups (1.9 L).

Note: Use a serrated peeler to most easily peel tomatoes, or follow the steps shown on page 43.

North Indian Ginger Soup Stock (*Adarak Masala*)

SLOW COOKER SIZE: 3½ QUART (3.32 L);
COOKING TIME: 10 HOURS ON HIGH; YIELD: 7 CUPS (1.66 L)

This is a unique take on a wet masala mixture. The story is that my grandfather's younger brother went on a religious retreat in India, where he was shown a preparation for what's now known in our family as Adarak (Ginger) Masala. We typically use it mixed with milk (Adarak ki Sabji, see recipe on page 156), but I've realized it's a fantastic base for most other dishes. For any dry or wet dish you make, you can heat this masala, mix in the main ingredient, and you're ready to eat—just like that!

2 large yellow onions, peeled (4 cups [600 g] ground)

2 pounds (908 g) ginger root, peeled (4 cups ground)

2 heaping cups (100 cloves) garlic, peeled, and trimmed (2 cups [300 g] ground)

4 tablespoons (24 g) cumin seeds

4 tablespoons (27 g) turmeric powder

½ cup (119 mL) oil

½ cup (119 mL) water

1. Grind the onions, ginger root, and garlic separately in a powerful blender, such as a Vitamix. The key is to grind each ingredient as finely as possible. As you finish grinding each ingredient, put it into the slow cooker. There's no need to clean the blender jug between ingredients.

2. Add the cumin, turmeric, and oil to the slow cooker. (See page 47 for details on making this dish without a slow cooker.)

3. Clean the blender jug with the water and dump that into the slow cooker. Mix gently.

4. Cook on high for 10 hours. This mix will last up to 1 week in the fridge and up to 3 months in the freezer. To use the *masala*, in a heavy pan, mix 1 cup (237 mL) in 1 teaspoon of hot oil as a base for just about any Indian-inspired meal (essentially eliminating the need to chop and add onion, ginger root, and garlic!). Add 2 cups (300 g) of beans, lentils, or any chopped vegetable. Add 1 teaspoon each of coarse sea salt and red chile powder or cayenne to taste. If you want a curried liquid base, add 2 cups (474 mL) water as well and heat the mixture through before serving. For our super-secret family recipe using this *masala*, take a look at *Adarak ki Sabji* on page 156.

To make this dish in a 5-quart (4.74-L) slow cooker, double all the ingredients and follow the above steps. Cook on high for 10 hours. Makes 14 cups (3.32 L).

Cashew Cream

YIELD: 2½ CUPS (593 ML)

The first time I ran across cashew cream was at a raw food restaurant owned by Karyn Calabrese, a prominent raw foodist in Chicago. It was so light and delicious that I just had to find out how it was made. My friend Jaya will attest that I stalked our waiter until he gave me the recipe. This is a terrific vegan option that replaces cream made from dairy in any Indian meal. You can use it to add a robust flavor to a lentil dish, or maybe give some depth to your rajmah, or you can mix it into spiced and stir-fried vegetables, such as mushrooms. Most nonvegans won't even notice the difference.

1 cup (138 g) raw cashews, soaked overnight and drained

1¼ cups (296 mL) water

1. Put the cashews in a powerful blender, such as a Vitamix. Add the water and blend on the highest speed until the mixture becomes smooth and creamy. If it's still too thick, add a little more water, 1 tablespoon at a time. Use it as a base for a nondairy alfredo sauce, or drizzle over steamed veggies.

Try This! Mix a few tablespoons of this cream into your red spaghetti sauce.

Tamarind Juice

YIELD: 4 CUPS (948 ML)

Making tamarind juice is likely every toddler's dream, because handling the pulp is without question messy—sticky and mushy! But if you persevere (or ask your little ones to start you out), you'll have liquid gold that is the tart and tangy base of most Indian chaats, tamarind rice, and even soups and drinks. Make up a batch and keep it on hand in the fridge for up to a month or in the freezer for even longer—just like soup stock.

1 (7-ounce [199-g]) block dried tamarind pulp with seeds

6 cups (1.42 L) boiling water

1. Cut the tamarind pulp into 1-inch (2.5-cm) pieces and place them in a deep bowl or saucepan. Be patient; it will stick to your knife, your fingers, and everything else. But don't worry—the mess is worth it!

2. Pour the boiling water over the pulp pieces. Let this sit for at least 1 hour.

3. With the back of a fork or your hands, break apart as much of the pulp as possible. Strain the liquid and store it, discarding the leftover pulp. It will keep in your refrigerator for up to a month. You can also freeze it for up to 3 months.

Ginger–Garlic Paste

YIELD: ¾ CUP (178 ML)

If you enjoy cooking Indian food but don't have time for much prep, this is a terrific shortcut. Just combine ginger root and garlic to create a paste that will last you up to a week in the fridge and up to 3 months in the freezer.

1 (4-inch [10-cm]) piece ginger root, peeled and chopped

12 cloves garlic, peeled and trimmed

1 tablespoon water

1. Process all the ingredients in a food processor until you have a paste-like consistency.

Try This! Put this paste into an ice-cube tray and freeze it. When you are ready to use some, just pop out a cube and set it aside to slightly defrost. I typically heat my oil, spices, and onions before adding this ginger-garlic paste to a dish. It's perfect to keep on hand for adding to a soup or stew. I love ginger for warding off coughs and garlic for preventing colds. Both are mainstays in my house. My girls have taken minced ginger root and garlic with water since they were old enough to swallow. Swallow a teaspoon of the above mixture with water as a great natural preventative to the most common cold ailments. If you have little ones, mix it with a spoonful of honey or agave nectar. My girls promise it works.

Baked, Spiced Tofu

YIELD: 2 CUPS (474 ML) BAKED AND CUBED

For most with authentic Indian tastes (my husband included), replacing homemade Indian cheese (paneer) with tofu is akin to blasphemy. I get it. There's a richness to paneer that seems irreplaceable to those who grew up on it. Indians have a lovefest with their dairy. Thus, my numerous attempts to substitute tofu for cheese in dishes such as mattar paneer and palak paneer were met with disdain at home until I discovered the art of baking tofu. This tiny step gives tofu a wonderful, almost meaty texture. Make a few batches, refrigerate them, and keep them on hand for anything and everything! Pure vegan magic.

Spray oil

2 teaspoons *garam masala* (optional)

1 (14-ounce [397-g]) package extra-firm organic tofu, sliced into ½-inch (13-mm) thick strips

1. Set an oven rack at the highest position, preheat your oven to 350°F (180°C), and lightly oil a baking sheet.

2. Sprinkle *garam masala* over one side of the tofu strips.

3. Place the tofu with the unseasoned side down on the baking sheet. Spray lightly with oil. Bake for 15 minutes. Flip the tofu slices, season them with the remaining *garam masala*, and spray lightly again with oil. Bake for another 15 minutes. Remove the pan from oven, let the tofu cool for 5 minutes, and cut it into cubes. Use the baked tofu immediately or store it for up to 1 week in an airtight container in the refrigerator for use later. You can also freeze it for up to 2 months.

Breakfast

Soaked Almonds

YIELD: 20 ALMONDS

It sounds a little bizarre to list something as simple as soaked almonds as a breakfast item. But in our house, it's an easy way to get protein and nutrients in the morning. My paternal grandmother was known for her amazing memory and attributed it to her habit of popping a few soaked almonds every morning. Soaking nuts also helps to break down an enzyme inhibitor they contain, which allows your body to absorb the nutrients more effectively and aids in digestion. Use a glass jar, if soaking overnight.

20 raw almonds

Water, for soaking

1. Soak almonds in enough water to cover them overnight.

2. In the morning, rinse well and either eat with the skin on or peel them and eat them. They are also great added to smoothies for a little protein boost. I often keep soaked almonds in my car and reach for them as a snack versus less healthy options.

Potato-Stuffed Bread
(*Aloo ka Parantha*)

YIELD: 12 (8-INCH [20-CM]) ROUNDS

Paranthas are the quintessential North Indian breakfast. As a kid, I'd wait for weekends when Mom would have time to make them, or visits to India when we'd eagerly look forward to being fed parantha *after* parantha *every morning. They'd arrive hot and steaming right off the tava to our plates. The best way to eat them is with a dollop of vegan butter on the side and a little bowl of soy yogurt sweetened with brown sugar or with some Indian pickle (achaar) on the side.*

4 medium potatoes, boiled, peeled, and mashed (4 cups [840 g])

1 tablespoon oil

1 heaping teaspoon cumin seeds

1 teaspoon turmeric powder

1 small yellow or red onion, peeled and minced (½ cup [75 g])

2–3 Thai, serrano, or cayenne chiles, stems removed, chopped

1 teaspoon red chile powder or cayenne

1 teaspoon mango powder (*amchur*)

1 tablespoon *garam masala*

2 teaspoons coarse sea salt

¼ cup (7 g) dried fenugreek leaves (lightly crushed to release flavor)

1 batch Basic *Roti* Dough (recipe follows)

1. Put the mashed potatoes in a deep bowl.

2. In a heavy pan, heat the oil over medium-high heat.

3. Add the cumin and turmeric, and cook until the seeds sizzle, about 30 seconds.

4. Add the onion and cook for 2 minutes, until slightly browned, stirring occasionally.

5. Add this mixture to the potatoes, along with the green chiles, red chile and mango powders, *garam masala*, salt, and fenugreek leaves. Mix everything together. I prefer to mix it by hand to make sure the potatoes are completely mashed. (Larger pieces of potato will break through your dough when you stuff it later. If you want to avoid touching the chiles, either use a large spoon or fork or wear kitchen gloves.)

6. Once the filling is finished, you can start rolling out the *roti* dough. Start by making Basic *Roti* Dough (recipe follows). Pull off a piece about the size of a golf ball (about 2 inches [5 cm] in diameter) and roll it between both palms to mold it into a ball. Press it between both palms to flatten it slightly, and roll it out on a lightly floured surface until it's about 5 inches (12.5 cm) in diameter.

7. Put a dollop (a heaping tablespoon) of the spicy potato filling right in the middle of the rolled-out dough. Fold in all sides so they meet in the middle—essentially making a square. Dip both sides of the square lightly in dry flour.

8. Roll it out on a surface lightly dusted with flour until it's thin and circular, about 10 inches (25 cm) in diameter. It may not be perfectly round, and some of the filling might come through slightly, but that's all OK.

9. Heat a *tava* or a heavy frying pan over medium-high heat. Once it's hot, place the *parantha* in the pan and heat for 30 seconds, until it's just firm enough to flip over but not completely hard or dried out. This step is critical to making really delicious *paranthas*. It will look like it's just about to cook but still a little raw. Cook for 30 seconds on the opposite side. Meanwhile, lightly oil the side that is facing up, flip it over, lightly oil the other side, and cook both sides until they brown slightly. Serve immediately with vegan butter, sweet soy yogurt, or Indian pickle (*achaar*).

Basic *Roti* Dough

3 cups (603 g) *chapati* flour (*atta*)

1½ cups (356 mL) water

1 tablespoon oil (optional)

1. Blend all the ingredients together in a food processor or by hand in a deep bowl until a ball forms.

Daikon-Stuffed Bread (Mooli ka Parantha)

YIELD: 12 (8-INCH [20-CM]) ROUNDS

My husband's favorite parantha is this one, which is stuffed with grated daikon. The key here is squeezing all the excess liquid out before stuffing the dough. These are so delicious that you'll make them over and over again.

1 (12-inch [30-cm] long) daikon radish, peeled and grated (4 cups [464 g])

1 teaspoon coarse sea salt

1–2 Thai, serrano, or cayenne chiles, stems removed, chopped

1 teaspoon *garam masala*

1 teaspoon red chile powder or cayenne

½ teaspoon turmeric powder

1 teaspoon ground ginger

1 teaspoon ground black pepper

1 teaspoon carom seeds (*ajwain*)

1 batch Basic *Roti* Dough (see recipe on page 73)

1. Place the radish and salt in a deep bowl. Let it sit for 15 minutes to pull out as much moisture as possible. Squeeze the excess water out of the radish. (I usually squeeze out a whole cup of liquid, so this step is important. Keep it to add to soup later.)

2. Add the chiles, *garam masala*, red chile powder, turmeric, ginger, black pepper, and carom. Mix well.

3. Once the filling is finished, start rolling out the *roti* dough. Start by making Basic *Roti* Dough. Pull off a piece about the size of a golf ball (about 2 inches [5 cm] in diameter) and roll it between both palms to mold it into a ball. Press it between both palms to flatten it slightly, and roll it out on a lightly floured surface until it's about 5 inches (12.5 cm) in diameter.

4. Put a dollop (a heaping tablespoon) of the spicy radish filling right in the middle of the rolled-out dough. Fold in all sides so they meet in the middle, essentially making a square. Dip both sides of the square lightly in dry flour.

5. Roll it out on a surface lightly dusted with flour until it's thin and circular, about 10 inches (25 cm) in diameter. It may not be perfectly round, and some of the filling might come through slightly, but that's all OK.

6. Heat a *tava* or a heavy frying pan over medium-high heat. Once it's hot, place the *parantha* in the pan and heat for 30 seconds, until it's just firm enough to flip over but not completely hard or dried out. This step is critical to making really delicious *paranthas*. It will look like it's just about to cook but still a little raw. Cook for 30 seconds on the opposite side. Meanwhile, lightly oil the side that is facing up, flip it over, lightly oil the other side, and cook both sides until they brown slightly. Serve immediately with vegan butter, sweet soy yogurt, or Indian pickle (*achaar*).

Cauliflower-Stuffed Bread (Gobi ka Parantha)

YIELD: 12 (8-INCH [20-CM]) ROUNDS

Freshly grated cauliflower tastes delicious stuffed into paranthas, and it's also incredibly nutritious. My young girls gobble these up whenever I make them.

2 cups (300 g) grated cauliflower (¼ head)

1 teaspoon coarse sea salt

½ teaspoon garam masala

½ teaspoon turmeric powder

1 batch Basic Roti **Dough (see recipe on page 73)**

1. In a deep bowl, mix together the cauliflower, salt, garam masala, and turmeric.

2. Once the filling is finished, start rolling out the roti dough. Start by making Basic Roti Dough. Pull off a piece about the size of a golf ball (about 2 inches [5 cm] in diameter) and roll it between both palms to mold it into a ball. Press it between both palms to flatten it slightly, and roll it out on a lightly floured surface until it's about 5 inches (12.5 cm) in diameter.

3. Put a dollop (a heaping tablespoon) of the cauliflower filling right in the middle of the rolled-out dough. Fold in all sides so they meet in the middle, essentially making a square. Dip both sides of the square lightly in dry flour.

4. Roll it out on a surface lightly dusted with flour until it's thin and circular, about 10 inches (25 cm) in diameter. It may not be perfectly round, and some of the filling might come through slightly, but that's all OK.

5. Heat a tava or a heavy frying pan over medium-high heat. Once it's hot, place the parantha in the pan and heat for 30 seconds, until it's just firm enough to flip over but not completely hard or dried out. This step is critical to making really delicious paranthas. It will look like it's just about to cook but still a little raw. Cook for 30 seconds on the opposite side. Meanwhile, lightly oil the side that is facing up, flip it over, lightly oil the other side, and cook both sides until they brown slightly. Serve immediately with vegan butter, sweet soy yogurt, or Indian pickle (achaar).

Note: If you have any extra cauliflower filling (which I always do), add chopped onion, green chiles, and some lemon juice and serve it as a side salad to any meal.

Spinach-Stuffed Bread

YIELD: 20–24 (5-INCH [12.5-CM]) ROUNDS

This was the very first parantha my girls got truly jazzed over. I'd make a batch and they'd take them rolled up everywhere—in the car, to the park, and to school. It was the easiest way to introduce my kids to spinach, a vegetable they've loved ever since. They especially love these paranthas because they turn a funky bright green after mixing in the food processor.

3 cups (603 g) 100% whole-wheat *chapati* **flour (***atta***)**

2 cups (60 g) fresh spinach, trimmed and finely chopped

1 cup (237 mL) water

1 teaspoon coarse sea salt

1. In a food processor, blend the flour and spinach. This will become a crumbly mixture.

2. Add the water and salt. Process until the dough becomes a sticky ball. If you don't have a food processor, you can mix the dough in a bowl by hand. I just find that my kids prefer the spinach mixed through the dough completely to make a green *parantha*. If you do it by hand, the spinach won't blend in as completely, but it will still taste delicious.

3. Transfer the dough to a deep bowl or to your lightly floured countertop and knead for a few minutes until it is smooth like pizza dough. If the dough is sticky, add a little more flour. If it's too dry, add a little more water.

4. Pull off a piece of the dough about the size of a golf ball (about 2 inches [5 cm] in diameter) and roll it between both palms to mold it into a ball. Press it between both palms to flatten it slightly, and roll it out on a lightly floured surface until it's about 5 inches (12.5 cm) in diameter.

5. Heat a *tava* or a heavy frying pan over medium-high heat. Once it's hot, place the *parantha* in the pan and heat for 30 seconds, until it's just firm enough to flip over but not completely hard or dried out. This step is critical to making really delicious *paranthas*. It will look like it's just about to cook but still a little raw. Cook for 30 seconds on the opposite side. Meanwhile, lightly oil the side that is facing up, flip it over, lightly oil the other side, and cook both sides until they brown slightly. Serve immediately with vegan butter, sweet soy yogurt, or Indian pickle (*achaar*). I love layering these *paranthas* for my kids with anything and everything from peanut butter and jelly to a slice of soy cheese and tofu. It's a perfect on-the-go breakfast or snack.

Try This! Swap out the spinach for mixed greens—anything from kale to beet greens.

Savory Cracked Wheat with Cashews (Upma [Uppama])

YIELD: 3 CUPS (711 ML)

I've been making this South Indian breakfast dish since I was in high school. My mother learned the recipe from a friend, and I passed it along to my best friend, Grace. Despite moving to Israel and having three kids, Grace makes this dish regularly for breakfast. I remember my mom serving it to my younger brother with mashed banana on the side, while I liked eating it with toast. Regardless of how you eat it, you'll love making this dish for your friends and family for breakfast, as a snack, and even for dinner.

1 cup (160 g) cracked wheat

1 tablespoon oil

1 teaspoon black mustard seeds

4–5 curry leaves, coarsely chopped

½ medium yellow or red onion, peeled and diced (½ cup [75 g])

1 small carrot, peeled and diced (¼ cup [32 g])

½ cup (145 g) peas, fresh or frozen (defrost first)

1–2 Thai, serrano, or cayenne chiles, stems removed, chopped

¼ cup (35 g) raw cashews, dry roasted

1 teaspoon coarse sea salt

2 cups (474 mL) boiling water

Juice of 1 medium lemon

1. In a heavy sauté pan over medium-high heat, dry roast the cracked wheat for about 7 minutes, until it is slightly browned. This is an important step, as it gives the dish depth and prevents the cracked wheat from becoming soggy later. Transfer to a plate to cool.

2. Heat the oil in a deep, heavy pan over medium-high heat.

3. Add the mustard seeds and cook until they sizzle, about 30 seconds.

4. Add the curry leaves, onion, carrot, peas, and chiles. Cook for 2 to 3 minutes, stirring occasionally, until the onions start to brown slightly.

5. Add the cracked wheat, cashews, and salt. Mix well.

6. Add the boiling water to the mixture. Do this very carefully, as it will splash. I take the lid for the large pan and hold it in front of me with my right hand while pouring the water with my left. As soon as the water is in there, I replace the lid and let the mixture settle down for a minute. Alternatively, you can turn the heat off temporarily while you pour in the water.

7. Once the water is in, reduce the heat to low and cook the mixture without the lid until all of the liquid is absorbed, stirring occasionally.

8. Add the lemon juice at the very end of the cooking time. Put the lid back on the pan, turn the heat off, and let the mixture sit for 15 minutes to better absorb all the flavors. Serve immediately with toast spread with vegan butter, mashed banana, or spicy green chile pepper chutney.

Note: This dish is traditionally made with cream of wheat. I subbed the cracked wheat to make it more nutritious. Try it the traditional way, which is delicious as well. Alternatively, you can substitute quinoa—just be sure to cook it first and skip the first step that calls for dry roasting.

South Indian Crêpes (Dosas)

YIELD: 3½ CUPS (830 ML) OF BATTER, MAKES ABOUT 24 MEDIUM-SIZED DOSAS

Dosas are absolutely the tastiest and healthiest breads around. A mainstay of the South Indian diet, these savory "crêpes" are traditionally made from white rice. In our home, where whole grains are the mainstay, we've switched it up a bit and always used brown rice. This switch gives you a heartier and a slightly darker dosa that I find to be much more filling and nutritious. This savory pancake is often eaten for breakfast or brunch, and that's why it appears in this section. Nonetheless, feel free to have them for dinner or as a snack. My girls love how they taste and have even learned to make them themselves (with a little supervision).

1 cup (190 g) brown basmati rice, cleaned and washed

¼ cup (48 g) whole black lentils with skin (*sabut urad dal*), cleaned and washed

2 tablespoons split gram (*chana dal*)

½ teaspoon fenugreek seeds

1 teaspoon coarse sea salt, divided

1½ cups (356 mL) water

Oil, for pan frying, set aside in a small bowl

½ large onion, peeled and halved (for prepping the pan)

1. In a large bowl, soak the rice in ample water.

2. In a separate bowl, soak the black lentils, split gram, and fenugreek.

3. Add ½ teaspoon salt to each bowl. Place each bowl in a warm area (I like to keep them in an oven that's turned off) with a loose lid and soak overnight.

4. In the morning, drain and reserve the water.

5. Grind the lentils and rice together in a powerful blender, such as a Vitamix. Add up to 1½ cups (356 mL) of water as you go. (You can use the reserved soaking water.)

6. Let the batter sit for 6 to 7 hours in a slightly warm place (again, such as an oven that's been turned off) to ferment slightly.

7. Heat a griddle over medium-high heat. Put 1 teaspoon of oil in the pan and spread it out with a paper towel or dish towel.

8. Once the pan is hot, stick a fork into the uncut, rounded part of the onion. Holding the fork handle, rub the cut half of the onion back and forth across your pan. The combination of the heat, the onion juices, and the oil will help prevent your *dosa* from sticking. I learned this from a South Indian family friend, Parvati Auntie, and it truly makes all the difference in the world. Keep the onion with the inserted fork handy to use again between *dosas*.

9. Keep a tiny bowl of oil on the side with a spoon, you'll use it later.

10. Now, finally on to the cooking! Ladle about ¼ cup (59 mL) of batter into the middle of the hot, prepped pan. With the back of your ladle, slowly make clockwise motions from the middle to the outer edge of the pan until it the batter becomes thin and crêpe-like.

11. With a small spoon, pour a thin stream of oil in a circle around the batter.

12. Let the *dosa* cook until it is slightly browned and pulls away from the pan slightly. Flip and cook the other side. Once it is browned, serve immediately layered with spiced *jeera* or lemon potatoes, coconut chutney, and a side of *sambhar*.

Chickpea Flour Crêpes (*Besan Poora*)

YIELD: 8 (5-INCH [12.5-CM] ROUND) PANCAKES

Usually, these thin North Indian pancakes are served with tea or a snack and eaten with a dollop of Indian pickle (achaar). When I was growing up, my mother made them for breakfast. They were easy, nutritious, and exceptionally delicious. I now make these for my girls as a wonderfully healthy protein-filled meal or snack. Keep the batter handy—it will last for up to a week in the fridge.

2 cups (184 g) gram (chickpea) flour (*besan*)

1½ cups (356 g) water

1 small onion, peeled and minced (about ½ cup [75 g])

1 (1-inch [2.5-cm]) piece ginger root, peeled and grated or minced

1–3 green Thai, serrano, or cayenne chiles, stems removed, chopped

¼ cup (7 g) dried fenugreek leaves (*kasoori methi*)

½ cup (8 g) fresh cilantro, minced

1 teaspoon coarse sea salt

½ teaspoon ground coriander

½ teaspoon turmeric powder

1 teaspoon red chile powder or cayenne

Oil, for pan frying

1. In a deep bowl, mix the flour and water until smooth. I like to start off with a whisk and then use the back of a spoon to break down the small clumps of flour that normally form.

2. Let the mixture sit for at least 20 minutes.

3. Add the remaining ingredients, except the oil, and mix well.

4. Heat a griddle over medium-high heat.

5. Add ½ teaspoon of oil and spread it over the griddle with the back of a spoon or a paper towel. You can also use a cooking spray to evenly coat the pan.

6. With a ladle, pour ¼ cup (59 mL) of the batter into the center of the pan. With the back of the ladle, spread the batter in a circular, clockwise motion from the center toward the outside of the pan to create a thin, round pancake about 5 inches (12.5 cm) in diameter.

7. Cook the *poora* until slightly brown on one side, about 2 minutes, and then flip it to cook on the other side. Press down with the spatula to ensure that the middle is also cooked through.

8. Cook the remaining batter, adding oil as needed to prevent sticking.

9. Serve with a side of my Mint or Peach Chutney (see recipes on pages 219 and 222) and Indian pickle (*achaar*) or make some hash browns spiced with cumin and use them as a filling. The possibilities are endless with this recipe. Try jazzing up the batter by folding in anything from mashed or grated potatoes to grated zucchini, chopped spinach, mint, or scallions.

Try This! My mother loves making this in the Vitamix blender so that all the ingredients combine really well and you get a smoother *poora*. Add the water first, then the remaining ingredients, and blend on the highest speed until smooth. I prefer a little crunch, so I like to add another ½ diced onion to the batter just before cooking.

Cream of Wheat Crêpes (*Rava Dosas*)

YIELD: 6 CUPS (1.42 L) OF BATTER, MAKES ABOUT 24 MEDIUM-SIZED *DOSAS*

This is the easiest and fastest way to make a dosa, the large, crispy, and savory "crêpes" made in South India. With this version, you don't have to soak anything overnight, nor do you have to let the batter sit for hours to ferment. It's a healthy and delicious savory pancake that your kids will love to eat. Fill it with anything and everything imaginable.

3 cups (534 g) cream of wheat (*sooji*)

2 cups (474 mL) unsweetened plain soy yogurt

3 cups (711 mL) water

1 teaspoon coarse sea salt

½ teaspoon ground black pepper

½ teaspoon red chile powder or cayenne

½ yellow or red onion, peeled and finely diced (½ cup [75 g])

1–2 green Thai, serrano, or cayenne chiles, stems removed, chopped

Oil, for pan frying, set aside in a small bowl

½ large onion, peeled and halved (for prepping pan)

1. In a deep bowl, mix together the cream of wheat, yogurt, water, salt, black pepper, and red chile powder and set it aside for 30 minutes to ferment slightly.

2. Add the diced onion and chiles. Mix gently.

3. Heat a griddle over medium-high heat. Put 1 teaspoon of oil in the pan.

4. Once the pan is hot, stick a fork into the uncut, rounded part of the onion. Holding the fork handle, rub the cut half of the onion back and forth across your pan. The combination of the heat, the onion juice, and the oil help prevent your *dosa* from sticking. Keep the onion with the inserted fork handy to use again between *dosas*. When it gets blackened from the pan, just thinly slice off the front.

5. Keep a tiny bowl of oil on the side with a spoon—you'll use it later.

6. Now, finally on to the cooking! Ladle a little more than ¼ cup (59 mL) of batter into the middle of your hot, prepped pan. With the back of your ladle, slowly make clockwise motions from the middle to the outer edge of the pan until the batter becomes thin and crêpe-like. If the mixture immediately starts to bubble, just turn your heat down slightly.

7. With a small spoon, pour a thin stream of oil in a circle around the batter.

8. Let the *dosa* cook until it is slightly browned and pulls away from the pan. Flip and cook the other side. Once it is browned, serve it immediately alone, with a side of coconut chutney, or layered with spiced *jeera* or lemon potatoes. You can simply serve it with Indian pickle (*achaar*) as well.

Try This! Mix up the veggies as much as you want. Anything from tomatoes, to bell peppers, to grated ginger root and chopped fresh cilantro will work. The possibilities are endless.

Note: Use regular cream of wheat, not the fast-cooking kind.

Homemade Soy Yogurt (*Dhai*)

SLOW COOKER SIZE: 3½ QUART (3.32 L); COOKING TIME: 13½ HOURS TOTAL, ON LOW AND WITH THE COOKER TURNED OFF; YIELD: 6 CUPS (1.42 L)

Although I've easily stayed away from dairy most of my adult life, yogurt has been the toughest habit to break. Savory raitas are such a strong part of our culinary culture that I truly didn't think it could be done. On top of this, most grocers who do sell soy yogurt offer only sweetened varieties. When I recently came across plain, unsweetened soy yogurt at my local Whole Foods Market in Chicago's Lincoln Park, I was immediately excited by the possibilities. I used the yogurt I purchased as my starter and made the recipe below. I think I did a little dance in my kitchen when I tasted the end product—it was delicious! Keep in mind, the results are a little thinner than standard yogurt purchased from the store, but it's still pretty darn good. The consistency is perfect for making Indian dishes and sides, including raitas, lassi, and khardi. Once you realize how much money you'll save making your own soy yogurt, you'll do a little dance too!

4 cups (948 mL) plain unsweetened soy milk

½ cup (119 mL) natural, live/active culture plain unsweetened soy yogurt

1 thick bath towel or blanket

1. Put the soy milk in the slow cooker and turn it on low. Cook for 2½ hours. (See page 47 for details on making this dish without a slow cooker.)

2. Unplug the slow cooker and let it sit for 3 hours with the cover on.

3. After 3 hours, transfer 2 cups (474 mL) of the lukewarm soy milk to a bowl and whisk in the live/active-culture yogurt. (This is basically any plain yogurt you have left over, either previously homemade yogurt or a store-bought version. Keep in mind that the yogurt you make will take on the taste and quality of the culture you are using, so don't use if it's old or sour.)

4. Return the mixture back to the slow cooker and stir gently.

5. Replace the lid and wrap the towel or blanket around the slow cooker to keep the contents warm. Let it sit for 8 hours. At this point, the yogurt should settle. Enjoy it blended into smoothies, with fruit, or made savory with grated veggies and salt and pepper. This also makes a wonderful base for *lassi*, an Indian yogurt-based drink.

To make this dish in a 5-quart (4.74-L) slow cooker, double the soy milk measurement (still using ½ cup (119 mL) of the live/active culture) and proceed with the recipe. A double recipe makes 10 cups (2.37 L).

Masala Tofu Scramble

YIELD: 2 CUPS (474 ML)

After a late night of partying, it's customary in India to hit the streets and eat spicy egg scramble with paranthas *(stuffed Indian bread). This is my vegan take on that spicy street omelette. My mom made it with real eggs, but as I've moved away from eating eggs, this has become a great substitute. I've converted many a carnivore with this dish!*

1 (14-ounce [397-g]) package extra-firm organic tofu

1 tablespoon oil

1 teaspoon cumin seeds

½ small white or red onion, peeled and minced (⅓ cup [50 g])

1 (½-inch [13-mm]) piece ginger root, peeled and grated or minced

1–2 green Thai, serrano, or cayenne chiles, stems removed, chopped

½ teaspoon turmeric powder

½ teaspoon red chile powder or cayenne

½ teaspoon coarse sea salt

½ teaspoon black salt (*kala namak*)

¼ cup (4 g) fresh cilantro, minced

1. Crumble the tofu with your hands and set it aside.

2. In a heavy, flat pan, heat the oil over medium-high heat.

3. Add the cumin and cook until the seeds sizzle, about 30 seconds.

4. Add the onion, ginger root, chiles, and turmeric. Cook and brown for 1 to 2 minutes, stirring to prevent sticking.

5. Add the tofu and mix well to ensure that the entire mixture turns yellow from the turmeric.

6. Add the red chile powder, sea salt, black salt (*kala namak*), and cilantro. Mix well.

7. Serve with toast or rolled in a warm *roti* or *parantha* wrap.

Note: Black salt works great in this dish because it has a slight sulfuric odor and tastes of eggs. A little goes a long way, so use it sparingly.

Sweet Pancakes (*Mitha Poora*)

YIELD: 8 (6-INCH [15-CM] ROUNDS) PANCAKES

Hands down, these sweet (mitha) pancakes (poora) were my favorite breakfast growing up. Whenever Mom was making a batch, I'd sit down first with a plate ready and waiting. I'd eat so many, she'd actually have to cut me off so that my brother and father would get some. They are best served with a little Indian pickle (achaar) for a sweet, savory experience. My favorite is pickled red chile pepper, but any spicy pickle will do.

1 cup (201 g) 100% whole-wheat chapati flour (*atta*)

½ cup (100 g) jaggery (*gur*) (Sucanat or dried sugarcane juice also works)

½ teaspoon fennel seeds

1 cup (237 mL) water

1. Mix all the ingredients together in a deep bowl and let the batter sit for at least 15 minutes.

2. Heat a lightly oiled griddle or frying pan over medium-high heat. Pour or scoop the batter onto the griddle, using about ¼ cup (59 mL) for each *poora*. The trick is to spread the batter out slightly with the back of the ladle from the middle in a clockwise motion without thinning it out too much. Brown on both sides and serve piping hot (the only way to eat these).

Soups, Small Plates, Salads, and Sides

North Indian Tomato Soup (Tamatar ka Shorba)

YIELD: 6 CUPS (1.42 L)

If any soup reminds me of my days visiting India, it's this one. It was often served in little cups as we sat in the living rooms of various friends and family members—a great starter for the meal ahead. I love having it on hand now to sip between meals to curb my appetite in a delicious and wholesome way.

2 teaspoons oil

1 heaping teaspoon cumin seeds

½ teaspoon turmeric powder

4 medium tomatoes, peeled and roughly chopped (4 cups [640 g])

1 (2-inch [5-cm]) piece ginger root, peeled and grated or minced

3 cloves garlic, peeled and chopped

1–2 green Thai, serrano, or cayenne chiles, stems removed, chopped

¼ cup (4 g) chopped fresh cilantro

½ teaspoon red chile powder or cayenne

4 cups (948 mL) water

1 teaspoon coarse sea salt

½ teaspoon ground black pepper

Juice of ½ lime

2 tablespoons nutritional yeast (optional)

Croutons, for garnish

1. In a large soup pot, heat the oil over medium-high heat.

2. Add the cumin and turmeric and cook until the seeds sizzle, about 30 seconds.

3. Add the tomatoes, ginger root, garlic, chiles, cilantro, red chile powder, and water. Bring to a boil.

4. Reduce the heat to medium-low heat and simmer for about 15 minutes. Once the tomatoes are soft, process with an immersion blender until smooth. (Alternatively, transfer the soup to a traditional or more powerful blender, such as a Vitamix, process, and return it to the pot.)

5. Add the salt, black pepper, lime juice, and nutritional yeast, if using. Mix well and serve piping hot, garnished with croutons. Make this into a mini meal by adding a tablespoon of cooked brown or white basmati rice to each cup before serving.

Note: Use a serrated peeler to most easily peel tomatoes, or follow the steps shown on page 43.

Seitan Mulligatawny Soup

YIELD: 12 CUPS (2.84 L)

I had so much fun testing this soup. It's hearty, spicy, and healthy. You'll never even miss the meat—even according to my husband, who requested seconds and then thirds.

1 cup (192 g) dried red split (brown) lentils (*masoor dal*), cleaned and washed

8 cups (1.90 L) water

1 medium onion, peeled and roughly chopped (1 cup [150 g])

2 medium tomatoes, peeled and roughly chopped (1 heaping cup [160 g])

1 small potato, peeled and diced (1 cup [150 g])

1 tablespoon whole black peppercorns

1 teaspoon turmeric powder

1 (8-ounce [227-g]) package plain seitan, drained and cut into small pieces (2 cups)

2 teaspoons coarse sea salt

1 teaspoon ground black pepper

1 tablespoon gram (chickpea) flour (*besan*)

3 tablespoons oil

3 tablespoons Ginger–Garlic Paste (see recipe on page 67 or mince 1 [1-inch] (2.5-cm) piece ginger root and 6 cloves garlic)

2 teaspoons ground cumin

2 teaspoons ground coriander

1 teaspoon red chile powder or cayenne

Juice of 1 lemon

1. Put the lentils, water, onion, tomatoes, potato, peppercorns, and turmeric in a large, heavy soup pot. Bring to a boil over medium-high heat, and then reduce the heat to a simmer.

2. Cook partially covered for 20 minutes.

3. Meanwhile, mix together the seitan, salt, and ground black pepper.

4. When the soup is finished cooking, blend it until smooth either with an immersion blender, a regular blender, or a more powerful blender, such as a Vitamix. Blend in batches if needed.

5. Lightly sprinkle the seitan with gram flour.

6. In a small frying pan, heat the oil over medium-high heat.

7. Add the Ginger–Garlic Paste and fry for 1 to 2 minutes. (Have a lid handy; the oil may splatter. Keep stirring, and lower the heat if needed.)

8. Add the cumin, coriander, and red chile powder and stir for 1 minute.

9. Add the seitan mixture and cook for another 3 minutes, until slightly browned.

10. Add this mixture to the soup, and bring to a boil.

11. Add the lemon juice.

12. Serve piping hot, in bowls. You can also add a tablespoon of cooked rice to each bowl before adding the soup for added texture.

Note: Use a serrated peeler to most easily peel tomatoes, or follow the steps shown on page 43.

Try This! For a fun, quick side, lose the soup and just prep the seitan (using half the salt). Once it's fried up, serve it with a side of rice or with *roti* or *naan*. I sometimes serve it as an appetizer, with toothpicks on the side. If you want to make this recipe gluten free, you can substitute baked tofu or tempeh for the seitan.

Spiced Green Soup (*Hara Shorba*)

YIELD: 8 CUPS (1.90 L)

This soup always reminds me of our visits to my Suraj Massi (maternal aunt) in Delhi during the winter—specifically, of coming back to her house after a long day of sightseeing, chilled and tired. She'd have this soup ready for us to sip out of a mug. It was like getting wrapped in a blanket—at once warm and comforting. For the leafy greens, use anything you might have lying around in the fridge. This is a great soup to serve as a starter to a meal or in between meals, when you're looking for a low-calorie, yet filling and nutritious, snack.

2 tablespoons oil

1 teaspoon cumin seeds

2 cassia leaves (or bay leaves)

1 medium yellow onion, peeled and roughly chopped (1 cup [150 g])

1 (1-inch [2.5-cm]) piece ginger root, peeled and grated or minced

10 cloves garlic, peeled and roughly chopped

1 small potato, peeled and roughly chopped (1 cup [150 g])

1–2 green Thai, serrano, or cayenne chiles, stems removed, chopped

2 cups (290 g) peas, fresh or frozen

2 cups (60 g) packed chopped greens (spinach, kale, beet or mustard greens, or a mix)

6 cups (1.42 L) water

½ cup (8 g) chopped fresh cilantro

2 teaspoons coarse sea salt

½ teaspoon ground coriander

½ teaspoon Roasted Ground Cumin (see recipe on page 62)

Juice of ½ lemon

Croutons, for garnish

1. In a deep, heavy soup pot, heat the oil over medium-high heat.

2. Add the cumin seeds and cassia leaves and heat until the seeds sizzle, about 30 seconds.

3. Add the onion, ginger root, and garlic. Cook for another 2 minutes, mixing occasionally.

4. Add the potato and cook for another 2 minutes.

5. Add the chiles, peas, and greens. Cook 1 to 2 minutes, until the greens have wilted.

6. Add the water. Bring to a boil, turn down the heat, and simmer uncovered for 5 minutes.

7. Add the cilantro.

8. Remove the cassia or bay leaves and blend with an immersion blender or in a traditional or a more powerful blender, such as a Vitamix, until smooth. Do this in two batches if you need to get it completely smooth.

9. Return the soup to the pot. Add the salt, coriander, and ground cumin.

10. Return the soup to a boil. Add the lemon juice and serve piping hot in mugs. Add croutons for some texture.

Note: Make sure your ginger root is fresh. Otherwise, when you blend the soup, the ginger threads won't break down as well to create a smooth texture. My daughter Neha alerted me to this on my first batch, but she loved the soup when I used fresher ginger root. Alternatively, you can use thinly sliced ginger root, which can be removed and discarded before blending the soup.

South Indian Tomato and Tamarind Soup (*Rasam*)

SLOW COOKER SIZE: 3½ QUART (3.32 L);
COOKING TIME: 4 HOURS ON HIGH; YIELD: 12 CUPS (2.84 L)

This soup is a mainstay in most South Indian households. The unique and tangy flavor comes from the combination of tomatoes and tamarind. I experimented with several recipes shared with me by family friends, only to find them complicated. They'd have you soak or pressure cook the lentils, then cook the tomatoes separately, and then make the tempering (tarka) on the side. I honestly didn't have time for that, so I turned to my slow cooker and was pleasantly surprised to find that it actually worked!

½ cup (96 g) dried split and skinned pigeon peas (*toor dal*), cleaned and washed

4 medium tomatoes, peeled and roughly chopped (4 cups [640 g])

1 (1-inch [2.5-cm]) piece ginger root, peeled and grated or minced

2 teaspoons coarse sea salt

1 teaspoon turmeric powder

1 cup (237 mL) Tamarind Juice (see recipe on page 66)

2 tablespoons *Rasam* Powder (see recipe on page 61)

7 cups (1.66 L) water

1 tablespoon oil

1 teaspoon black mustard seeds

1 teaspoon cumin seeds

15–20 curry leaves, roughly chopped

1 heaping tablespoon chopped fresh cilantro, for garnish

Lemon wedges, for garnish

1. Put the pigeon peas, tomatoes, ginger root, salt, turmeric, Tamarind Juice, *Rasam* Powder, and water in the slow cooker. Cook on high for 3½ hours. (See page 47 for details on making this dish without a slow cooker.)

2. Blend with an immersion blender, in a traditional blender, or in a powerful blender, such as a Vitamix.

3. Meanwhile, on the stovetop, make the tempering (*tarka*). In a sauté pan, heat the oil over medium-high heat. Add the mustard and cumin and cook until the mixture sizzles, about 30 seconds. Add the curry leaves and cook until the leaves turn slightly brown and begin to curl. Be careful to mix occasionally so the spices don't burn. After 1 to 2 minutes, put the hot mixture into the slow cooker.

4. Cook the soup for another 30 minutes and serve immediately, garnished with the cilantro and a lemon wedge. I love serving this in a shot glass with grated lemon zest for parties.

Note: Use a serrated peeler to most easily peel tomatoes, or follow the steps shown on page 43. If you don't have time to prepare Tamarind Juice, substitute 1 to 2 teaspoons tamarind paste for 1 cup juice. And if you don't have *Rasam* Powder handy, no worries. The soup is still delicious without it. To get the traditional thin, broth-like consistency, peeling the tomatoes is key. You can also strain the soup before serving.

To make this dish in a 5-quart (4.74-L) slow cooker, double all the ingredients except the water (use 10 cups (2.37L) and follow the above steps. Cook on high for 4½ hours, blend, and cook for another 30 minutes. Makes 21 cups (4.98 L). Yes, your slow cooker will be very full, but don't worry—it won't overflow.

Spiced Stovetop Popcorn

YIELD: 10 CUPS (2.37 L)

I am always shocked by how many of my friends think popcorn can only be made in the microwave. I grew up making it on the stove, and so will my girls. They love pouring the oil and the corn kernels, and then hearing them pop. It also tastes much better spiced with Indian masalas than with heavy butter.

1 tablespoon oil

½ cup (100 g) uncooked popcorn kernels

1 teaspoon coarse sea salt

1 teaspoon *garam masala, Chaat Masala* **(see recipe on page 57) or** *Sambhar Masala* **(see recipe on page 60)**

1. In a deep, heavy pan, heat the oil over medium-high heat.

2. Add the popcorn kernels.

3. Cover the pan and turn the heat to medium-low.

4. Cook until the popping sound slows down, 6 to 8 minutes.

5. Turn off the heat and let the popcorn sit with the lid on for another 3 minutes.

6. Sprinkle with the salt and *masala*. Serve immediately.

Papad

YIELD: 6–10 WAFERS

Also known as papadum *in South India, these thin, wafer-like crisps are typically made from lentil, potato, rice, or gram (chickpea) flour (besan). In North India, they are usually eaten as a light snack with drinks before a meal—the same idea as beer nuts. You purchase the uncooked, dried wafers at an Indian grocer in various flavors, from plain to mild to spicy. My young girls absolutely adore the extra-spicy version made from ground black pepper, watching it crisp up on the stovetop and then crushing it by hand over soft lentils and rice just like I did as a kid.*

1 package store-bought *papad* (made from lentils)

1. With tongs, take one *papad* at a time and heat it over the stovetop. If you have a gas stove, cook it right over the flame, being careful to blow out the bits that catch fire. Constantly flip them back and forth until all parts are cooked and crisp. If using an electric stove, heat them on a wire rack set over the burner and flip continuously until they are crisped. Be careful—they burn easily.

2. Stack the *papads* and serve immediately as a snack or with dinner.

Note: A quick shortcut is to cook these in the microwave on a plate. Usually a minute will do the trick, but the time will vary depending on your microwave. In restaurants, *papads* are deep fried until crispy, though they taste just as good if not better made on the stovetop.

Masala Papad

YIELD: 6–10 WAFERS

Making a little spicy topping for your papad is something I came across years ago, when I was a staffer on Capitol Hill, while eating at a D.C. Indian restaurant. It's a fun and unique way to present a traditional Indian snack, and it's become a favorite for my kids.

1 (6–10 count) package store-bought *papad* (made from lentils)

2 tablespoons oil

1 medium red onion, peeled and minced (1 cup [150 g])

2 medium tomatoes, diced (1 cup [160 g])

1–2 green Thai, serrano, or cayenne chiles, stems removed, finely sliced

1 teaspoon *Chaat Masala* (see recipe on page 57)

Red chile powder or cayenne, to taste

1. With tongs, take one *papad* at a time and heat it over the stovetop. If you have a gas stove, cook it right over the flame, being careful to blow out little bits that catch fire. The best way to cook these is to constantly flip them until all parts are cooked and crisp. If using an electric stove, heat them on a wire rack set over the burner and flip continuously until they are crisped. Be careful—they burn easily.

2. Lay the *papads* out on a large tray.

3. With a pastry brush, lightly brush each *papad* with oil.

4. In a small bowl, mix together the onion, tomatoes, and chiles.

5. Spoon 2 tablespoons of the onion mixture over each *papad*.

6. Top off each *papad* with a sprinkle of *Chaat Masala* and red chile powder. Serve immediately.

Note: Because these need to be eaten immediately, garnish each *papad* just before serving.

Roasted *Masala* Nuts

YIELD: 4 CUPS (948 ML)

This is probably one of the easiest ways to impress your party guests. I love making up a batch of mixed spiced nuts before dinner parties and placing them around the house in small, silver Indian bowls. Yes, these mixtures can be purchased from an Indian grocer, but when you make them at home, they only have the salt and oil that you've included. Post party, they're a great after-school treat for the kids (and you).

2 cups (276 g) raw cashews

2 cups (286 g) raw almonds

1 tablespoon *garam masala, Chaat Masala* **(see recipe on page 57) or** *Sambhar Masala* **(see recipe on page 60)**

1 teaspoon coarse sea salt

1 tablespoon oil

¼ cup (41 g) golden raisins

1. Set an oven rack at the highest position and preheat the oven to 425°F (220°C). Line a baking sheet with aluminum foil for easy clean up.

2. In a deep bowl, mix together all the ingredients except the raisins until the nuts are evenly coated.

3. Arrange the nut mixture in a single layer on the prepared baking sheet.

4. Bake for 10 minutes, mixing gently halfway through the cooking time to ensure that the nuts cook evenly.

5. Remove the pan from the oven. Add the raisins and let the mixture cool for at least 20 minutes. This step is important. Cooked nuts become chewy, but they get their crunchiness back once they've cooled. Serve immediately or store in an airtight container for up to a month.

Note: Get as creative as you want with the spicing. I've seen these nuts cooked with everything from simple ground black pepper and sea salt, to red chile pepper, to the *masalas* listed above.

Chai-Spiced Roasted Almonds and Cashews

YIELD: 4 CUPS (948 ML)

I developed this recipe while I was testing my Roasted Masala Nuts (see recipe on page 96). You can get chai just about anything else, so why not nuts? It was a perfect pairing, and one that I make regularly now. I love cooking up batches around the holidays. Sealed in pretty pouches, they make a perfect and unique gift.

2 cups (276 g) raw cashews

2 cups (286 g) raw almonds

1 tablespoon *Chai Masala* **(see recipe on page 56)**

1 tablespoon jaggery (*gur*) or brown sugar

½ teaspoon coarse sea salt

1 tablespoon oil

1. Set an oven rack at the highest position and preheat the oven to 425°F (220°C). Line a baking sheet with aluminum foil for easy clean up.

2. In a deep bowl, combine all the ingredients and mix well until the nuts are evenly coated.

3. Arrange the nut mixture in a single layer on the prepared baking sheet.

4. Bake for 10 minutes, mixing halfway through the cooking time to ensure that the mixture cooks evenly.

5. Remove the baking sheet from the oven and let the mixture cool for about 20 minutes. This step is important. Cooked nuts become chewy, but they get their crunchiness back once they've cooled. Serve immediately or store in an airtight container for up to a month.

Spicy Bean Salad (*Chana Chaat*)

YIELD: 5 CUPS (1.19 L)

I've been making fresh chickpea chaat ever since I first ate it by the lake in Chandigarh. There's just something about the perfect, irresistible mix of veggies, spices, and heat. Then, of course, the sweet and sour of the tamarind chutney really brings it home. It makes you want to lick your fingers and the bowl clean—the exact meaning of the Hindi word chaat itself. Feel free to substitute any bean or lentil for the chickpeas—black chickpeas, black-eyed peas, lima beans, and even kidney beans. What I love about this salad the most is that if you look down the list of ingredients, you won't see any oil or unnecessary fats. All of the flavor comes from the spices and lemon juice.

---

4 cups cooked beans (or 2 [15-ounce] (426-g) cans, drained and rinsed)

1 medium potato, boiled and diced (1 cup [150 g])

½ medium red onion, peeled and diced (½ cup [75 g])

1 medium tomato, diced (1 cup [160 g])

1 (1-inch [2.5-cm]) piece ginger root, peeled and grated or minced

2–3 green Thai, serrano, or cayenne chiles, stems removed, chopped

Juice of 1 lemon

1 teaspoon black salt (*kala namak*)

1 teaspoon *Chaat Masala* (see recipe on page 57)

½ teaspoon coarse sea salt

½–1 teaspoon red chile powder or cayenne

¼ cup (4 g) chopped fresh cilantro

¼ cup (59 mL) Tamarind–Date Chutney (see recipe on page 224)

1. In a large bowl, mix together all the ingredients except the Tamarind–Date Chutney.

2. Divide the salad among small serving bowls and top each off with a tablespoon of Tamarind–Date Chutney.

Note: Because of the combination of lemon juice and tomatoes, this salad doesn't have a long shelf life. Some recipes call for you to mix in the Tamarind–Date Chutney, but I prefer to add it at the end. It tends to make the salad soggy if it's mixed in too early.

Try This! My cousin Ashok in Delhi insists that the best way to mix your *chaat* is the way the street vendors do it. Take a bowl equal in size to your mixing bowl and place it upside down on top of the mixing bowl so that there are no openings where the rims to meet. Then, shake away. He claims it's the only way to distribute the juices and spices evenly. I've tried it and I'm totally convinced!

Roasted *Masala* Cauliflower and Broccoli with Tomatoes

YIELD: 8 CUPS (1.90 L)

Although broccoli rarely makes it to the Indian dinner table, it is grown in India. I grew up visiting my grandmother's home in Chandigarh, where the gardener (mali) always planted a row of broccoli plants at the far end of the front garden. Likely, it was more for show, but I'd often walk over, pluck off a floret, and munch on it right then and there. I was determined to include broccoli (one of my kids' favorite veggies) in this book. This recipe worked perfectly.

1 large head cauliflower, florets removed and sliced into bite-size pieces (3 cups [300 g])

1 large head broccoli, florets removed and sliced into bite-sized pieces (1 cup [100 g])

2 cups (320 g) cherry tomatoes

1 heaping tablespoon *garam masala*

2 teaspoons coarse sea salt

2 tablespoons oil

1. Set an oven rack at the highest position and preheat the oven to 425°F (220°C). Line a baking sheet with aluminum foil for easy clean up.

2. Put the cauliflower, broccoli, and tomatoes in a large, roomy bowl.

3. Add the *garam masala*, salt, and oil. Mix gently.

4. Arrange the mixture on the prepared baking sheet. Cook for 30 minutes, stirring once halfway through the cooking time. Let cool slightly.

5. Serve with rice, stuffed in a pita, or with *roti* or *naan*.

Chickpea Poppers

YIELD: 4 CUPS (948 ML)

I first heard about chickpea poppers from my friend Chasity Santoro, a fellow mom at my kids' school who shares my passion for feeding her kids healthy food. I'd never thought to bake chickpeas with Indian spices because I was so used to making them into a chana masala dish. The first time I made these, my kids went utterly crazy, not only gorging themselves on them that night, but also asking me to put them in their lunch boxes the next day. I now make a batch and set it aside for quick snacks, as a substitute for croutons on my salad, and as a nice addition to soups. The best is watching the kids in front of the television popping these into their mouths instead of chips and junk food. I love serving them with a side of Tamarind–Date or Mint Chutney (see recipes on pages 224 and 219).

4 cups cooked chickpeas (see recipe on page 128) or 2 (12-ounce [341-g]) cans chickpeas

1 tablespoon *garam masala, Chaat Masala* (see recipe on page 57) or *Sambhar Masala* (see recipe on page 60)

2 teaspoons coarse sea salt

2 tablespoons oil

1 teaspoon red chile powder, cayenne pepper, or paprika, plus more for sprinkling

1. Set an oven rack at the highest position and preheat the oven to 425°F (220°C). Line a baking sheet with aluminum foil for easy clean up.

2. Drain the chickpeas in a large colander for about 15 minutes to get rid of as much moisture as possible. If using canned, rinse first.

3. In a large bowl, gently mix together all the ingredients.

4. Arrange the seasoned chickpeas in a single layer on the baking sheet.

5. Cook for 15 minutes. Carefully take the tray out of the oven, mix gently so that the chickpeas cook evenly, and cook another 10 minutes.

6. Let cool for 15 minutes. Sprinkle with the red chile powder, cayenne pepper, or paprika.

Roasted Eggplant Dip (*Baingan Bharta*)

YIELD: 5 CUPS (1.19 L)

Although it's typically eaten with a meal, bharta also makes a great dip. I discovered this at a signing for my first book at the Olive Tap in Long Grove, Illinois. I was late and busy prepping my station while customers started to come toward my table looking for food. I quickly laid out some crackers and what that day became Roasted Eggplant Dip. It was done "help yourself" style and was a huge hit. Guests at your next party will think you slaved over your stovetop for hours to roast the eggplant just so, never realizing how simple it is to make such a healthy and creative dish.

3 medium eggplants with skin (the large, round, purple variety)

2 tablespoons oil

1 heaping teaspoon cumin seeds

1 teaspoon ground coriander

1 teaspoon turmeric powder

1 large yellow or red onion, peeled and diced (2 cups [300 g])

1 (2-inch [5-cm]) piece ginger root, peeled and grated or minced

8 cloves garlic, peeled and grated or minced

2 medium tomatoes, peeled (if possible) and diced (1 cup [160 g])

1–4 green Thai, serrano, or cayenne chiles, stems removed, chopped

1 teaspoon red chile powder or cayenne

1 tablespoon coarse sea salt

1. Set an oven rack at the second-highest position. Preheat the broiler to 500°F (260°C). Line a baking sheet with aluminum foil to avoid a mess later.

2. Poke holes in the eggplant with a fork (to release steam) and place them on the baking sheet. Broil for 30 minutes, turning once. The skin will be charred and burnt in some areas when they are done. Remove the baking sheet from the oven and let the eggplant cool for at least 15 minutes. With a sharp knife, and cut a slit lengthwise from one end of each eggplant to the other, and pull it open slightly. Scoop out the roasted flesh inside, being careful to avoid the steam and salvage as much juice as possible. Place the roasted eggplant flesh in a bowl—you'll have about 4 cups (948 mL).

3. In a deep, heavy pan, heat the oil over medium-high heat.

4. Add the cumin and cook until it sizzles, about 30 seconds.

5. Add the coriander and turmeric. Mix and cook for 30 seconds.

6. Add the onion and brown for 2 minutes.

7. Add the ginger root and garlic and cook for 2 more minutes.

8. Add the tomatoes and chiles. Cook for 3 minutes, until the mixture softens.

9. Add the flesh from the roasted eggplants and cook for another 5 minutes, mixing occasionally to avoid sticking.

10. Add the red chile powder and salt. At this point, you should also remove and discard any stray pieces of charred eggplant skin.

11. Blend this mixture using an immersion blender or in a separate blender. Don't overdo it—there should still be some texture. Serve with toasted *naan* slices, crackers, or tortilla chips. You can also serve it traditionally with an Indian meal of *roti*, lentils, and *raita*.

Tofu Chickpea Fritters (*Tofu Pakora*)

YIELD: ABOUT 12 PAKORAS

One of the most amazing food memories I have is a visit we paid to a hill station in North India with my family. There, we were served hot paneer fritters with steaming cups of chai as an afternoon snack. Making them with tofu won't leave you feeling deprived, but it will leave you wanting more!

1 (14-ounce [397-g]) package extra-firm organic tofu, sliced ¼ inch (6 mm) thick and the slices cut in 2-inch (5-cm) squares

2 cups (184 g) gram (chickpea) flour (*besan*)

1 (1-inch [2.5-cm]) piece ginger root, peeled and grated or minced

¼ cup (7 g) loosely packed dried fenugreek leaves (*kasoori methi*), crushed gently to release flavor (optional)

1 teaspoon coarse sea salt

½ teaspoon *garam masala*

½ teaspoon red chile powder or cayenne

½ teaspoon ground black pepper

1 teaspoon carom seeds (*ajwain*)

1¼ (296 mL) cups water

Oil, for pan frying

1. Boil the sliced tofu in water for about 5 minutes. Drain it a colander while you prep the remaining ingredients. Alternatively, you can also freeze the tofu either in the package or after cutting. Once you defrost, proceed with the steps below. I found that the two processes essentially give you the same flavor and texture. You can also use the tofu as is, but the added step will add a richness to the tofu that will make it taste more like Indian cheese, or *paneer*.

2. In a bowl, combine the flour, ginger root, fenugreek (if using), salt, *garam masala*, red chile powder, black pepper, and carom.

3. Slowly mix in the water a little at a time, and keep stirring until the mixture becomes a slightly thick, smooth paste.

4. In a griddle or frying pan, heat the oil over medium-high heat.

5. As the oil is heating, dip 3 to 4 pieces of tofu in the gram flour mixture until each is entirely coated.

6. Take each piece out slowly with a fork, allowing the excess to drip off. Slowly place each piece in the pan. Cook until browned on one side, then flip and cook until the other side is browned. To ensure that the edges are also cooked, cover the pan for 30 seconds to a minute.

7. Serve immediately with ketchup or homemade mint chutney. This is a great filling for a pita pocket or as a vegan answer to a burger.

Baked Veggie Squares (*Tukri Pakora*)

YIELD: 25 MEDIUM-SIZED SQUARES

My mom has been making this baked take on a traditional fried Indian snack for years. My challenge was to come up with a vegan version that would forgo the traditional yogurt. My first batch, made without any yogurt or tofu substitute, was too dense. Thank goodness for silken tofu. It did the trick, making for a healthy snack that I can feel really good about feeding to my family.

2 cups (140 g) grated white cabbage (½ small head)

1 cup (100 g) grated cauliflower (¼ medium head)

1 cup (124 g) grated zucchini

½ potato, peeled and grated (½ cup [75 g])

½ medium yellow or red onion, peeled and diced (½ cup [75 g])

1 (1-inch [2.5-cm]) piece ginger root, peeled and grated or minced

3–4 green Thai, serrano, or cayenne chiles, stems removed, chopped

¼ cup (4 g) minced fresh cilantro

3 cups (276 g) gram (chickpea) flour (*besan*)

½ (12-ounce [341-g]) package silken tofu

1 tablespoon coarse sea salt

1 teaspoon turmeric powder

1 teaspoon red chile powder or cayenne

¼ teaspoon baking powder

¼ cup (59 mL) oil

1. Set an oven rack at the middle position and preheat the oven to 350°F (180°C). Oil a 10-inch (25-cm) square baking pan. Use a larger baking pan if you want a thinner, crispier *pakora*.

2. In a deep bowl, combine the cabbage, cauliflower, zucchini, potato, onion, ginger root, chiles, and cilantro.

3. Add the flour and mix slowly until well combined. It helps to use your hands to really blend everything together.

4. In a food processor, blender, or a more powerful blender, such as a Vitamix, blend the tofu until smooth.

5. Add the blended tofu, salt, turmeric, red chile powder, baking powder, and oil to the vegetable mixture. Mix.

6. Pour the mixture into the prepared baking pan.

7. Bake for 45 to 50 minutes, depending on how warm your oven gets. The dish is finished when a toothpick inserted into the middle comes out clean.

8. Cool for 10 minutes and cut into squares. Serve with your favorite chutney.

Spicy Sweet Potato Patties (*Aloo Tikki*)

YIELD: 10 MEDIUM-SIZED PATTIES

Street food is some of the most addictive and delicious of Indian foods. Vendors all over India make potato patties, which are pan-fried like hamburgers and served over a toasted bun or slice of bread. You'll be shocked by how easy they are to make at home and how delicious they are even when you substitute sweet potatoes for white potatoes. I love frying these up fresh as a quick and healthy after-school snack for my girls. Remember, you want to eat them piping hot for the best flavor.

1 large sweet potato (or white potato), peeled and cut into ½-inch (13-mm) dice (about 4 cups [600 g])

3 tablespoons (45 mL) oil, divided

1 teaspoon cumin seeds

½ medium yellow or red onion, peeled and finely diced (½ cup [75 g])

1 (1-inch [2.5-g]) piece ginger root, peeled and grated or minced

1 teaspoon turmeric powder

1 teaspoon ground coriander

1 teaspoon *garam masala*

1 teaspoon red chile powder or cayenne

1 cup (145 g) peas, fresh or frozen (defrost first)

1–2 green Thai, serrano, or cayenne chiles, stems removed, chopped

1 teaspoon coarse sea salt

½ cup (46 g) gram (chickpea) flour (*besan*)

1 tablespoon lemon juice

Chopped fresh parsley or cilantro, for garnish

1. Steam the potato until soft, about 7 minutes. Let it cool. Use your hands or a potato masher to gently break it down. You'll have about 3 cups (630 g) mashed potatoes at this point.

2. In a shallow frying pan, heat 2 tablespoons of the oil over medium-high heat.

3. Add the cumin and cook until it sizzles and is slightly browned, about 30 seconds.

4. Add the onion, ginger root, turmeric, coriander, *garam masala*, and red chile powder. Cook until soft, another 2 to 3 minutes. Let the mixture cool.

5. Once it has cooled, add the mixture to the potatoes, followed by the peas, green chiles, salt, gram flour, and lemon juice.

6. Mix well with your hands or large spoon.

7. Form the mixture into small patties and set them aside on a tray.

8. In a large, heavy pan, heat the remaining 1 tablespoon of oil over medium-high heat. Cook the patties in batches of 2 to 4, depending on the size of the pan, for about 2 to 3 minutes per side, until browned.

9. Serve hot, garnished with the chopped fresh parsley or cilantro. This patty can be eaten as a sandwich, on a bed of lettuce, or as a fun side to your entrée. The mixture will keep for about 3 to 4 days in the fridge. To make the more traditional patty, use regular potatoes in place of the sweet potatoes.

Note: To add a little more protein, mix in some cooked or canned chickpeas or black beans. You can also mix in other greens, such as chopped spinach or kale. Or, give the dish a little South Indian flavor by substituting black mustard seeds for the cumin and frying up fresh curry leaves.

Baked Samosas

YIELD: 12 MEDIUM SAMOSAS

Though samosas are the quintessential Indian snack food, they are also packed with fat and calories because they are traditionally fried. My family and I love to eat samosas as a snack once in a while, but we usually avoid them because of all the extra calories. The pastry is usually also made from processed all-purpose white flour, which is a turn-off for me as someone who tries to go for only whole foods and grains. I was determined to find a way to make an everyday baked samosa from whole-wheat flour. Even my hardcore Punjabi father gave me a thumbs-up for the result.

DOUGH:

1 cup (201 g) 100% whole-wheat *chapati* flour

½ teaspoon coarse sea salt

3 tablespoons (45 mL) oil

4 tablespoons (60 mL) water

FILLING:

1 tablespoon oil

1 teaspoon cumin seeds

1 teaspoon turmeric powder

1 medium onion, peeled and diced (1 cup [150 g])

1 green Thai, serrano, or cayenne chile, stem removed, finely sliced

½ heaping cup (73 g) peas, fresh or frozen

½ teaspoon *garam masala*

½ teaspoon ground coriander

½ teaspoon red chile powder or cayenne

½ teaspoon mango powder (*amchur*)

1 teaspoon coarse sea salt

2 large potatoes, peeled and finely diced (2 cups [300 g])

1. In a food processor, blend together the flour, salt, and oil. (If you don't have a food processor, just do this by hand.)

2. Add the water. Process for another 2 to 3 minutes. The dough will be a little crumbly.

3. Transfer the dough to a deep bowl, and mix by hand until you have a smooth ball. Add more water in tiny amounts, if needed.

4. Wrap the ball of dough tightly in plastic wrap so it does not dry out. Let it sit for 30 minutes.

5. To make the filling: In a heavy pan, heat the oil over medium-high heat.

6. Add the cumin and cook until the seeds sizzle, about 30 seconds.

7. Add the turmeric, onion, and chile. Cook until the onion is browned, about 2 minutes, stirring occasionally to prevent sticking.

8. Add the peas, *garam masala*, coriander, red chile and mango powders, salt, and potatoes. Cook 2 to 3 minutes, stirring occasionally.

9. Turn the heat to low and partially cover the pan. Cook for 10 to 15 minutes, until the potatoes are softened.

10. Remove the pan from the heat, remove the lid, and let the mixture cool completely. If you fill the dough with a warm mixture, it will melt.

11. To fill the samosas: Lightly oil a baking sheet, or line it with aluminum foil. Set an oven rack at the middle position. Preheat the oven to 425°F (220°C) Have a small bowl of water handy. Pull off a small ball of dough, the size of a quarter. Roll it thin, into a circle about 6 inches (15 cm) in diameter. This part is key. The thinner you can get it (without the filling pushing through later), the crispier your samosa will be. While you are rolling out the dough, keep the remaining portion in plastic wrap or under a slightly damp paper towel to help keep it moist.

12. With a sharp knife, slice the circle in half, making 2 half-moon shapes. This will make 2 samosas.

13. Dip your finger in the bowl of water and moisten the edge of the straight side.

14. Pick up one edge of the half circle and bring it to the other edge, creating an ice-cream cone shape. Gently press the moistened edges together with your fingers to seal.

15. With your other hand, take a heaping tablespoon of the potato filling and gently stuff it into the open end of the cone.

16. Wet the open inside edges of the dough. Seal them together gently. You should now have a filled triangle!

17. Gently place the triangle on the prepared baking sheet.

18. Continue rolling, cutting, molding, and filling until you've used all the dough.

19. To bake the samosas: Brush both sides of the samosas lightly with oil, or spray them with cooking spray.

20. Bake the samosas for 10 minutes.

21. Gently flip the samosas over and bake for another 7 to 8 minutes, until slightly browned. Transfer the samosas to a tray to cool slightly before serving with a side of Mint and/or Tamarind–Date Chutneys (see recipes on pages 219 and 224).

Notes: The type of flour you use is key here. Most *chapati* flour is a soft, finely milled whole-wheat flour. In the West, hard red wheat flour is popular, which is slightly bitter in taste and darker in color than *chapati* flour. To make a lighter, tastier pastry, opt for the *chapati* flour, which can be found in any Indian grocery store. If you don't have access to an Indian grocer, track down some whole-wheat pastry flour, which can be found in most specialty health food stores. If you can't find that, mix 2 parts traditional whole-wheat flour with 1 part all-purpose white flour.

My mother is adamant that the potatoes be diced finely and cooked on the stovetop rather than boiled first, to avoid them becoming mashed. Finely dicing them also prevents the filling from pushing through the pastry when you fill the samosas.

Baked Samosa Sticks

YIELD: 12 MEDIUM SAMOSA STICKS

Making homemade samosas is a cinch, especially when you forgo the traditional triangle pocket and instead just roll the pastry into a samosa stick. I find traditionally shaped samosas difficult to eat. The shape is awkward, and they're usually too big and intimidating for my kids. When you opt for the cocktail-sized samosas, you get more dough than filling and total disappointment. These samosa sticks are not only fun to make—they're also fun to eat. Your kids will go crazy over them just like mine did.

DOUGH:

1 cup (201 g) 100% whole-wheat *chapati* flour

½ teaspoon coarse sea salt

3 tablespoons (45 mL) oil

4 tablespoons (60 mL) water

FILLING:

1 tablespoon oil

1 teaspoon cumin seeds

½ teaspoon turmeric powder

1 small onion, peeled and minced (½ cup [75 g])

1 green Thai, serrano, or cayenne chile, stem removed, finely sliced

½ cup (73 g) peas, fresh or frozen (defrost first)

½ teaspoon *garam masala*

½ teaspoon ground coriander

½ teaspoon red chile powder or cayenne

½ teaspoon mango powder (*amchur*)

1 teaspoon coarse sea salt

3 medium potatoes, peeled, diced, boiled, and slightly mashed

1. In a food processor, blend together the flour, salt, and oil. (If you don't have a food processor, just do this by hand.)

2. Add the water. Process for another 2 to 3 minutes. The dough will be a little crumbly.

3. Transfer the dough to a deep bowl, and mix by hand until you have a smooth ball. Add more water in tiny amounts, if needed.

4. Wrap the ball of dough tightly in plastic wrap so it does not dry out. Let it sit for 30 minutes.

5. In a heavy sauté pan, heat the oil over medium-high heat.

6. Add the cumin and cook until the seeds sizzle, about 30 seconds.

7. Add the turmeric, onion, and chile. Cook until the onion is browned, about 2 minutes, stirring occasionally to prevent sticking.

8. Add the peas, *garam masala*, coriander, red chile and mango powders, salt, and potatoes. Cook 2 to 3 minutes, stirring occasionally.

9. Turn the heat to low and partially cover the pan. Cook for another 2 to 3 minutes. When the mixture is heated through, mash the potatoes with the back of a large spoon until they are broken down. If you have large pieces of potato, they will push through the pastry later.

10. Remove the pan from the heat, remove the lid, and let the mixture cool completely. If you fill the dough with a warm mixture, it will melt.

11. To roll the samosas: Lightly oil a baking sheet or line it with aluminum foil. Position a rack in the middle of the oven. Preheat the oven to 425°F (220°C). Pull off a small ball of dough, about a teaspoon. The smaller you can keep it, the better. Roll it thin, into a circle about 3 to 4 inches (7.5 to 10 cm) in diameter. This part is key. The thinner you can get the dough (without getting it so thin that the filling

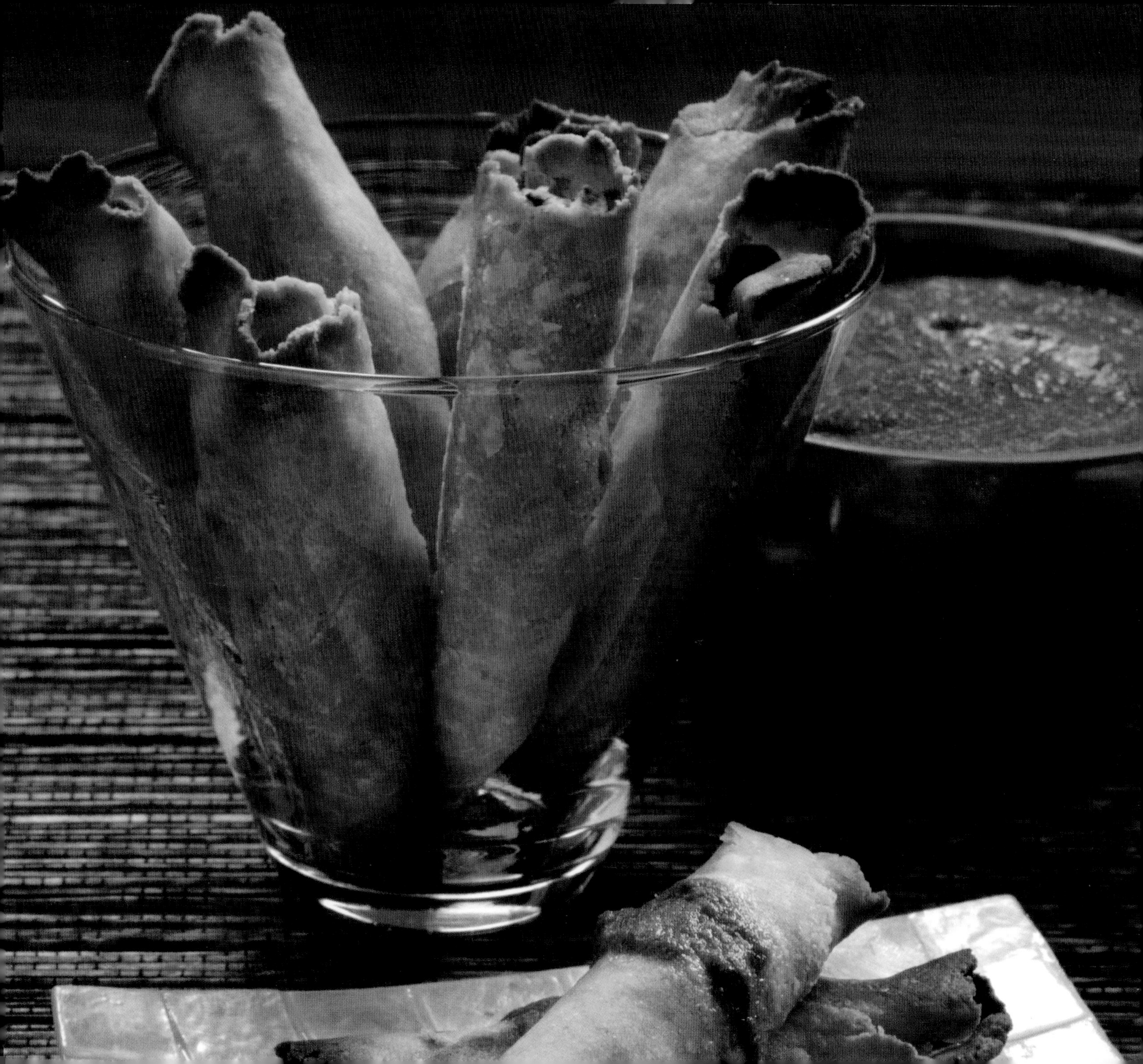

pushes through later), the crispier your samosa. While you are rolling out the dough, keep the remaining portion in plastic wrap or under a slightly damp paper towel to help keep it moist. If the dough sticks to the rolling pin, lightly coat your rolling pin with cooking spray or lightly spray your dough.

12. Take about a tablespoon of the filling and spread it in over the pastry, leaving a ¼-inch (6-mm) border.

13. Take the edge closest to you and slowly and carefully roll it toward the opposite edge. Press softly to seal. Because of the oil in the dough, it should seal easily. The filled tube should be about 3 to 4 inches (7.5 to 10 cm) long, a perfect size for little fingers. Sometimes the dough is too thin and sticks to your surface as you try to roll it. Just keep a spatula or a butter knife handy to gently help you lift the edge. Once you have that up, you'll be able to roll the rest easily.

14. Gently place the filled and rolled sticks seam-side down on the prepared baking sheet.

15. Continue until you finish assembling all of your samosa sticks.

16. To bake the samosas: Brush or spray all sides of the samosa sticks lightly with oil.

17. Bake the samosa sticks for 7 to 10 minutes.

18. Gently flip them over, and bake for another 7 to 8 minutes, until lightly browned.

19. Transfer the sticks to a tray to cool slightly before serving with a side of Mint and/or Tamarind–Date Chutneys (see recipes on pages 219 and 224).

Notes: The type of flour you use is key here. Most *chapati* flour is a soft, finely milled whole-wheat flour. In the West, hard red wheat flour is popular, which is slightly bitter in taste and darker in color than *chapati* flour. To make a lighter, tastier pastry, opt for the *chapati* flour, which can be found in any Indian grocery store. If you don't have access to an Indian grocer, track down some whole-wheat pastry flour, which can be found in most specialty health food stores. If you can't find that, mix 2 parts traditional whole-wheat flour with 1 part all-purpose white flour.

This samosa filling needs to have a mashed-potato texture, because you will be rolling it. If you use a mixture with large pieces or chunks, they will push through the dough when rolling.

If you are storing these to serve later, let them cool completely before you put them into an airtight container, or you run the risk of the crust getting slightly soft rather than staying crispy. Heat them in a traditional oven or toaster oven before serving for best results.

Sprouts

Sprouting is the process of germinating seeds, which when soaked and allowed to sprout are high in enzymes and nutrition. Keep in mind that you can only sprout whole legumes. Once they've been split or processed, you've eliminated the seeds' ability to absorb water and grow. Whole green lentils (sabut moong) are some of the easiest and tastiest to sprout. My kids will eat handfuls of them raw out of the fridge. In India, sprouting is not seen as the exotic tradition it is in the West; it's an everyday process, and sprouted salads are commonly eaten.

1 cup whole beans or lentils, cleaned and washed

1. Soak the beans or lentils in water overnight.

2. In the morning, drain them completely. Lightly dampen a paper towel or dishcloth and place it on a plate or tray. Spread the beans or lentils in a single layer on this paper towel or dishcloth and set the plate in a warm spot for the day, such as a toaster oven or regular oven (that's been turned off). It will take a day or two for the beans or lentils to begin sprouting.

3. Keep the beans or lentils damp by sprinkling them with water, being careful not to get them too wet. Once they've sprouted, transfer the sprouts in an air-tight glass container and refrigerate them for up to a week.

Note: An important tip for green lentils is to sift through them after they are soaked and sprouted. There will often be a few hard ones left behind that won't soften. Remove these before proceeding with the recipe that follows. You can try this process with just about any whole lentil or bean, including brown lentils (*masoor*), black lentils (*urad*), chickpeas, black chickpeas (*kala chana*), and fenugreek seeds. Avoid kidney beans, as they release toxins when they sprout and should not be eaten in this form.

Mom's *Mung* Sprout Salad

YIELD: 2 CUPS (474 ML)

During one of my summer visits to my mother's home in King of Prussia, Pennsylvania, my mother pulled out all of her recipes, which were handwritten on index cards and slips of paper in a green, rusting metal box. This was one of the recipes she held up proudly and called her own. Now you can make it your own, too.

1 cup (192 g) sprouted whole green lentils (*sabut moong*)

1 green onion, chopped

1 small tomato, chopped (½ cup [80 g])

½ small red or yellow bell pepper, chopped (¼ cup [38 g])

1 small cucumber, peeled and chopped (½ cup [65 g])

1 small potato, boiled, peeled, and chopped (½ cup [75 g])

1 (1-inch [2.5-cm]) piece ginger root, peeled and grated or minced

1–2 green Thai, serrano, or cayenne chiles, stems removed, chopped

¼ cup (4 g) chopped fresh cilantro

Juice of ½ lemon or lime

½ teaspoon sea salt

½ teaspoon red chile powder or cayenne

½ teaspoon oil

1. Combine all the ingredients and mix well. Serve as a side salad or as a quick, healthy, high-protein snack. Stuff inside a pita with a chopped avocado for a quick lunch.

Tomato, Cucumber, and Onion Salad (*Kachumber*)

YIELD: 5 CUPS (1.19 L)

My Tripta Auntie introduced me to this salad years ago, and I can't get enough of it. So simple to make and yet such complex flavors. You might even get into my habit of sipping the last bits of lime out of the bowl when the salad is finished, like I do. Shhhh…don't tell anyone!

1 large yellow or red onion, peeled and diced (1 heaping cup [150 g])

4 medium tomatoes, diced (2 cups [320 g])

4 medium cucumbers, peeled and diced (2 cups [260 g])

1–3 green Thai, serrano, or cayenne chiles, stems removed, chopped

Juice of 2 limes

¼ cup (4 g) chopped fresh cilantro

1 teaspoon coarse sea salt

1 teaspoon black salt (*kala namak*)

1 teaspoon red chile powder or cayenne

1. In a large bowl combine all the ingredients and mix well. Serve immediately as a side to any dish, or serve with a side of chips as a quick and healthy salsa. Keep in mind that with the combination of lime and tomatoes, this salad does not have a long shelf life.

Sharon's Veggie Salad Sandwiches

YIELD: 4 SANDWICHES

When I was growing up, my best friend and neighbor Sharon Flynn and I loved swapping cultures. I visited her house across the street for a traditional Thanksgiving every year, while she would come over for Indian food. One of our favorite pastimes was sitting on my front lawn and making sandwiches out of Indian-seasoned vegetables. I'd get a huge plate filled with sliced tomatoes, bell peppers, and onions doused with lemon juice. Then we'd sit there for hours, pile them up, and eat them. Surely all the neighbors on Anthony Road thought we were crazy!

1 large tomato, cut in thick slices

1 large bell pepper, thinly sliced into rings

1 large red onion, peeled and thinly sliced into rings

Juice of 1 lemon

½ teaspoon coarse sea salt

½ teaspoon black salt (*kala namak*)

1. Arrange the vegetables on plate with tomatoes first, then peppers, and onion rings layered on top.

2. Sprinkle the vegetables with the lemon juice, sea salt, and black salt.

3. Serve immediately. Sitting on your front lawn and making sandwiches is optional.

Chickpea Popper Street Salad (*Chana Chaat*)

YIELD: 5 CUPS (1.19 L)

The streets of India are filled with food carts. These delicious side plates are called chaat, *a Hindi word that essentially means to lick your fingers clean. I assembled this recipe one night when I needed a quick dish for dinner.*

4 cups (948 mL) Chickpea Poppers (see recipe on page 100) cooked with any *masala*

1 medium yellow or red onion, peeled and diced (1 cup [150 g])

1 large tomato, diced (1 cup [160 g])

Juice of 2 lemons

½ cup (8 g) chopped fresh cilantro

2–4 green Thai, serrano, or cayenne chiles, stems removed, chopped

1 teaspoon coarse sea salt

1 teaspoon black salt (*kala namak*)

1 teaspoon red chile powder or cayenne

1 teaspoon *Chaat Masala* (see recipe on page 57)

½ cup (119 mL) Mint Chutney (see recipe on page 219)

½ cup (119 mL) Tamarind–Date Chutney (see recipe on page 224)

1 cup (237 mL) Soy Yogurt *Raita* (see recipe on page 124)

1. In a deep bowl, mix together the Chickpea Poppers, onion, tomato, lemon juice, cilantro, chiles, sea salt, black salt, red chile powder, and *Chaat Masala.*

2. Divide the mixture among individual serving bowls.

3. Top each bowl with a tablespoon each of Mint and Tamarind–Date Chutneys and Soy Yogurt *Raita.* Serve immediately.

Street Corn Salad (*Bhutta*)

YIELD: 4 CUPS (948 ML)

I'll never forget the day I created a slice of my favorite part of Delhi visits in my mother's kitchen in King of Prussia, Pennsylvania. I'm not sure what led me to try, but I took a few ears of corn, put a little metal rack over an electrical burner on my mom's stovetop, and laid 2 ears of corn on it. I turned the burner on high and waited to see what would happen. After roasting the cobs to a beautiful shade of dark brown–black, I compiled spices in a little bowl, sliced lemons, and took the tray up to my parents' bedroom. They were in heaven. Today, I like to cut off the kernels and make a side salad as an afterschool treat for my girls. This recipe was included in the Chicago Sun-Times' *list of most memorable recipes for 2010.*

4 ears corn, husked and cleaned

Juice of 1 medium lemon

1 teaspoon coarse sea salt

1 teaspoon black salt (*kala namak*)

1 teaspoon *Chaat Masala* (see recipe on page 57)

1 teaspoon red chile powder or cayenne

1. Roast the corn until slightly charred. This can be done many ways. I simply do it right on my stovetop. I have gas burners, so I turn them to medium-high and roast 2 ears at a time, turning them slightly as they roast. If you have an electric stove, you can do the same, but put a small metal rack over your burner so that the corn does not sit directly on it and make a mess. If you don't want to go this route (though I find it to be the simplest), you can roast the corn on a grill.

2. Remove the kernels from the corn. Either use a fancy gadget designed for this purpose or do as I do—take a serrated knife, hold the cob with one hand, and work your way carefully down the length of the cob with the other hand (which is obviously holding the knife!).

3. Put the corn kernels in a bowl and mix in all the other ingredients. Serve immediately.

Try This! If you truly want to go traditional, put the spices in a small plate, and serve the ears of corn whole, accompanied by the spices and a lemon half. Have your guests pat the lemon (flat side down) in the plate of spices and rub the spiced lemon down their corn cobs until all of the corn is seasoned. Squeeze the lemon slightly as you go down the length of the corn to give it as much flavor as possible.

Note: If you wash the corn first, be sure to dry the cobs completely before putting them on the stovetop, or they will splatter when cooking. I learned this one the hard way.

Crunchy Carrot Salad

YIELD: 5 CUPS (1.19 L)

My kids love raw carrots, so we always have them in the house. This salad is an easy way to use them up. This salad delivers protein, too, with the addition of lentils.

½ cup (96 g) split and skinned green lentils (*yellow mung*), cleaned and washed

5 cups (550 g) peeled and grated carrots (about 8–9 medium)

1 medium daikon, peeled and grated (1 cup [114 g])

¼ cup (40 g) raw peanuts, dry roasted

¼ cup (4 g) minced fresh cilantro

Juice of 1 medium lemon

2 teaspoons coarse sea salt

½ teaspoon red chile powder or cayenne

1 tablespoon oil

1 heaping teaspoon black mustard seeds

6–7 curry leaves, roughly chopped

1–2 green Thai, serrano, or cayenne chiles, stems removed, chopped

1. Soak the lentils in boiled water for 20 to 25 minutes, until al dente. Drain.

2. Place the carrots and daikon in a deep bowl.

3. Add the drained lentils, peanuts, cilantro, lemon juice, salt, and red chile powder.

4. In a shallow, heavy pan, heat the oil over medium-high heat.

5. Add the mustard seeds. Cover the pan (so they don't pop out and burn you) and cook until the seeds sizzle, about 30 seconds.

6. Carefully add the curry leaves and green chiles.

7. Pour this mixture over the salad and mix well. Serve immediately, or refrigerate before serving.

Try This! If you can find fresh coconut, grate about 3 tablespoons (15 g) and add it at the end. If you use grated, unsweetened packaged coconut, fry it in the oil along with the curry leaves and chiles before adding it to the salad.

Pomegranate *Chaat*

YIELD: 3 CUPS (711 ML)

In our house, we love pomegranate season. There's nothing better than extracting the seeds yourself and eating them spiced with a touch of black salt (kala namak). Many folks balk at the idea of removing the seeds, but it's not as tough as it seems. Take the pomegranate in one hand and a rolling pin in the other. Tap the fruit with the rolling pin all around to loosen the seeds. Then slice the ends and cut the fruit in four pieces. Working over a large bowl, take the seeds out with your hand, removing the outside skin and the white membrane. Just be careful not to get the juice on your clothes—you may never get it out.

2 large pomegranates, seeds removed (3 cups [522 g])

½–1 teaspoon black salt (*kala namak*)

1. Mix the seeds with the black salt. Enjoy immediately, or refrigerate for up to a week.

Masala Fruit Salad (Fruit *Chaat*)

YIELD: 9–10 CUPS (2.13–2.37 L)

This is a wonderfully easy recipe, especially when you are trying to get through a bunch of fruit in the fridge. Just chop it all up, add some lemon juice and spices, and what looked boring before suddenly tastes like you've been transported to a street corner in India, where fruit chaat is regularly served. A basic recipe starts with a ripe cantaloupe, but use this recipe simply as a template for infinite combinations of fruit. The beauty of this recipe is that fruit does not have to be juicy sweet—even a bland cantaloupe will come to life with these spices. For the kids, leave out the red chile.

1 medium ripe cantaloupe, peeled and diced (7 cups [1.09 kg])

3 medium bananas, peeled and sliced (2 cups [300 g])

1 cup (100 g) seedless grapes

2 medium pears, cored and diced (2 cups [300 g])

2 small apples, cored and diced (1 cup [300 g])

Juice of 1 lemon or lime

½ teaspoon coarse sea salt

½ teaspoon *Chaat Masala* (see recipe on page 57)

½ teaspoon black salt (*kala namak*)

½ teaspoon red chile powder or cayenne

1. In large bowl, gently mix together all the ingredients. Serve immediately the traditional street food way, in small bowls with toothpicks.

Orange Salad

YIELD: 3½ CUPS (830 ML)

Believe it or not, oranges are also considered a street food in parts of India. When they're in season, you'll see vendors positioned around bustling marketplaces and office buildings squeezing fresh juice from large, juicy oranges. They mix this juice with a dash of salt and black salt (kala namak). The rest is history—delicious, sweet, tangy refreshment in a glass. This salad reminds me of the same taste. The olives are a Middle Eastern twist that gives you a real pop of flavor.

3 medium oranges, peeled, seeded, and diced (3 cups [450 g])

1 small yellow or red onion, peeled and minced (½ cup [75 g])

10–12 black kalamata olives, pitted and roughly chopped

¼ cup (4 g) chopped fresh cilantro

Juice of 2 medium limes

½ teaspoon coarse sea salt

½ teaspoon black salt (*kala namak*)

½ teaspoon *garam masala*

½ teaspoon ground black pepper

¼ teaspoon red chile powder or cayenne

1. Gently mix together all the ingredients. Refrigerate for at least 30 minutes before serving.

Brown Rice and Adzuki Bean *Dhokla*

YIELD: ABOUT 2 DOZEN SMALL SQUARES

Dhokla is a delicious snack food with roots in Gujarat, a state in western India. The light, airy, steamed squares are served with tea or as an appetizer at a party and are traditionally made with white rice and yogurt. I worked hard to develop a recipe that incorporated whole-grain brown rice and soy instead. I tried using only brown rice but got a very dense square that just wasn't all that fun to eat. Using brown and white rice delivers the perfect blend of whole-grain nutrition and the airiness of the traditionally made snack. My love for the food and culture of Japan led me to substitute adzuki beans for the traditional black lentils (urad dal). Try using either—you'll love the results.

½ cup (95 g) brown basmati rice, washed

½ cup (95 g) white basmati rice, washed

½ cup (99 g) whole adzuki beans with skin, picked over and washed

2 tablespoons split gram (*chana dal*)

¼ teaspoon fenugreek seeds

½ (12-ounce [341-g]) package soft silken tofu

Juice of 1 medium lemon

1 teaspoon coarse sea salt

1 cup (237 mL) water

½ teaspoon *eno* or baking soda

½ teaspoon red chile powder, cayenne, or paprika

1 tablespoon oil

1 teaspoon brown or black mustard seeds

15–20 curry leaves, roughly chopped

1–3 green Thai, serrano, or cayenne chiles, stems removed, sliced lengthwise

1. Soak the brown and white rice, adzuki beans, split gram, and fenugreek together in water overnight.

2. In a powerful blender, such as a Vitamix, combine the drained rice and lentil mixture, tofu, lemon juice, salt, and 1 cup water.

3. Grind on high for 4 to 5 minutes, until smooth. Be patient. You may need to stop and scrape down the sides of the jug so that it blends evenly. Pour the mixture into a deep bowl.

4. Let the batter sit for 2 to 3 hours. No more, or it will start to sour.

5. Oil a deep, square pan. (Mine is 9 inches [22.5 cm] square and 2 inches [5 cm] deep.)

6. Sprinkle the *eno* or baking soda across the bottom, and stir gently 2 or 3 times. You'll immediately see it start to bubble.

7. Pour the batter into the prepared pan.

8. Bring some water to a boil in a double boiler wide enough to fit your square pan. Place the square pan gently in the top section of the double boiler.

9. Cover the pan and steam for 12 to 15 minutes. The *dhokla* is cooked when a toothpick inserted into the middle comes out clean. Remove the lid and let it cool for 10 minutes in the pan.

10. Carefully remove the square pan from the double boiler.

11. Slowly cut the *dhokla* into squares and arrange them in a pyramid on a large plate.

12. Sprinkle them with the red chile, cayenne, or paprika.

13. Prepare the tempering. In a sauté pan, heat 1 tablespoon oil over medium-high heat. Add the mustard seeds. Once they begin to pop, add the curry leaves and chiles.

14. Pour this mixture evenly over the *dhokla*. Serve immediately with a side of mint-cilantro or coconut chutney.

Note: *Eno* is only found in specialty stores, such as Indian grocers. If you can't find it, use baking soda, which will work but won't create such an airy end product. If you don't have curry leaves, you can use chopped fresh cilantro.

Soy Yogurt *Raita*

YIELD: 1 CUP (237 ML)

Yogurt is a huge part of the Indian diet, but not sugary and sweet as it is eaten in the West. Indians traditionally add spices like roasted cumin and black salt to their yogurt, along with grated and/or chopped veggies, making a side of yogurt an incredibly healthy addition to a meal. This is the most basic recipe; feel free to add anything and everything from grated carrots to cooked and diced beets to diced daikon. Though lemon or lime juice is not traditionally added to raita, *it helps round out the flavor when using soy yogurt.*

1 cup (237 mL) plain, unsweetened soy yogurt

1 cucumber, peeled, grated, and squeezed to remove excess water

½ teaspoon Roasted Ground Cumin (see recipe on page 62)

½ teaspoon coarse sea salt

½ teaspoon black salt (*kala namak*)

½ teaspoon red chile powder

Juice of ½ lemon or lime

1. In a bowl, mix together all the ingredients. Serve immediately.

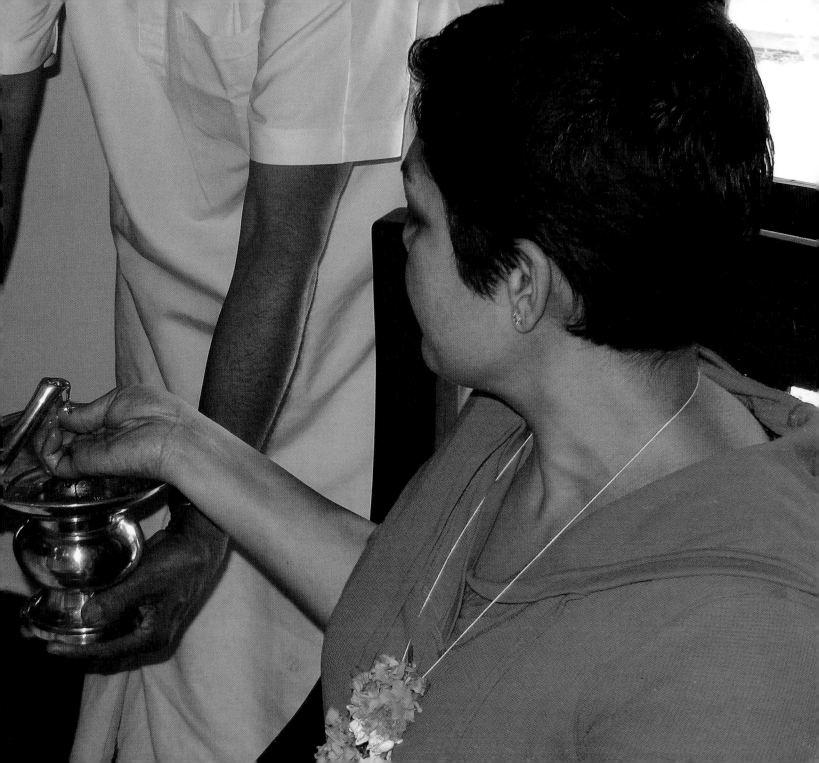

Slow-Cooked Legumes to Stovetop

WHEN MOST PEOPLE WANT TO USE BEANS OR WHOLE LENTILS IN A RECIPE, THEY usually reach for canned or frozen varieties. I insist on reaching for my slow cooker. With just a little planning, making wholesome, healthy, and salt-free beans and lentils can be a cinch, helping you to avoid more expensive cans and frozen options.

I'd also argue that you get a better, more nutritious product. Cooked dried beans taste better, absorb flavors better, and have a better texture than their canned counterparts, which I find to be slightly mushy. Though beans can be made on the stovetop, this process rarely works well for me because it requires vigilance—a luxury that, as a mom of two young girls, I just don't have. The water invariably evaporates while I'm upstairs with a kid in the bath, and by the time I remember, the pot is a charred mess. With the slow cooker, you avoid all the extra hazards and instead always end up with easy, cooked beans on hand to sprinkle into salads, add to soups, whip up homemade hummus, or make into delicious Indian meals in seconds. (See page 47 for details on making these dishes without a slow cooker.)

This section takes the pain and fuss out of making beans and lentils from dried varieties. Use the first set of recipes as your go-to whenever you plan to serve beans or lentils during the next week. Each of these recipes is for dried varieties cooked in water only. You'll end up with plain, cooked beans and lentils without the preservatives and salt of canned varieties and without the hassle of stovetop cooking.

Once they're cooked, go to the recipes that follow. They give you more than a dozen different and fun ways to prep 2 to 4 cups (396 to 792 g) of your cooked beans and lentils. Feel free to swap out any bean or lentil for any preparation style. For example, if you are making *Chana Chaat* (see recipe on page 98), start with a traditional chickpea preparation, but then try subbing black beans another week. You'll have a blast experimenting with all the possible options.

The beauty of it all? Nothing goes to waste. Take whatever plain beans or lentils you don't have a chance to use and stick them in the freezer. They'll keep for up to 3 months. You'll never scramble for takeout again.

Cooked, Plain Black Chickpeas (*Sookha Kala Chana*)

SLOW COOKER SIZE: 3½ QUART (3.32 L); COOKING TIME: 4 HOURS ON LOW; YIELD: 7 CUPS (1.66 L)

3 cups (681 g) whole, dried black chickpeas (*kala chana*), picked over and washed

5 cups (1.19 L) water

1. Put the chickpeas and water in the slow cooker. (See page 47 for details on making this dish without a slow cooker.)

2. Cook on low for 4 hours.

3. Rinse the beans in a colander with cold water to stop the cooking process and drain any excess liquid.

4. Store the beans in the refrigerator for up to 1 week or in the freezer up to 3 months.

To make this dish in a 5-quart (4.74-L) slow cooker, use 6 cups (1.36 kg) dried chickpeas and 8 cups (1.90 L) water. Cook on high for 4 hours. A double recipe makes 14 cups (3.32 L).

Cooked, Plain White Chickpeas (*Sookha Kabhuli Chana*)

SLOW COOKER SIZE: 3½ QUART (3.32 L); COOKING TIME: 4 HOURS ON HIGH; YIELD: 7 CUPS (1.66 L)

3 cups (681 g) whole, dried white chickpeas, picked over and washed

5 cups (1.19 L) water

1. Put the chickpeas and water in the slow cooker. (See page 47 for details on making this dish without a slow cooker.)

2. Cook on high for 4 hours.

3. Rinse the beans in a colander with cold water to stop the cooking process and drain any excess liquid.

4. Store the beans in the refrigerator for up to 1 week or in the freezer up to 3 months.

To make this dish in a 5-quart (4.74-L) slow cooker, use 6 cups (1.36 kg) dried chickpeas and 8 cups (1.90 L) water. Cook on high for 4 hours. A double recipe makes 14 cups (3.32 L).

Cooked, Plain Brown Lentils (*Sookha Sabut Masoor Dal*)

SLOW COOKER SIZE: 3½ QUART (3.32 L); COOKING TIME: 3 HOURS ON LOW; YIELD: 8 CUPS (1.90 L)

::

3 cups (576 g) whole brown lentils (*masoor dal*), picked over and washed

5 cups (1.19 L) water

1. Put the lentils and water in the slow cooker. (See page 47 for details on making this dish without a slow cooker.)

2. Cook on low for 3 hours.

3. Rinse the beans in a colander with cold water to stop the cooking process and drain any excess liquid.

4. Store the lentils in the refrigerator for up to 1 week or in the freezer up to 3 months.

To make this dish in a 5-quart (4.74-L) slow cooker, use 6 cups (1.15 kg) dried brown lentils and 8 cups (1.90 L) water. Cook on low for 3 hours. A double recipe makes 14 cups (3.32 L).

Cooked, Plain Black Beans

SLOW COOKER SIZE: 3½ QUART (3.32 L); COOKING TIME: 4 HOURS ON LOW; YIELD: 7 CUPS (1.66 L)

::

3 cups (681 g) whole, dried black beans, picked over and washed

5 cups (1.19 L) water

1. Put the black beans and water in the slow cooker. Cook on low for 4 hours. Cook a little longer if you want the beans to be softer. I prefer them al dente so they hold up in the freezer and in salads. (See page 47 for details on making this dish without a slow cooker.)

2. Rinse the beans in a colander with cold water to stop the cooking process and drain any excess liquid.

3. Store the beans in the refrigerator for up to 1 week and in the freezer up to 3 months. This will be a great base for salads, dips, *chaats*, and other dishes throughout the week.

To make this dish in a 5-quart (4.74-L) slow cooker, use 6 cups (1.36 kg) dried black beans and 8 cups (1.90 L) water. Cook on low for 5 hours. A double recipe makes 12 cups (2.84 L).

Cooked, Plain Black-Eyed Peas (*Sookha Lobhia*)

SLOW COOKER SIZE: 3½ QUART (3.32 L); COOKING TIME: 4 HOURS ON LOW; YIELD: 7 CUPS (1.66 L)

3 cups (681 g) whole, dried black-eyed peas, picked over and washed

5 cups (1.19 L) water

1. Put the black-eyed peas and water in the slow cooker. (See page 47 for details on making this dish without a slow cooker.)

2. Cook on low for 4 hours.

3. Rinse the beans in a colander with cold water to stop the cooking process and drain any excess liquid.

4. Store the beans in the refrigerator for up to 1 week or in the freezer up to 3 months.

To make this dish in a 5-quart (4.74-L) slow cooker, use 6 cups (1.36 kg) dried black-eyed peas and 8 cups (1.90 L) water. Cook on low for 3½ hours. A double recipe makes 13 cups (3.08 L).

Cooked, Plain Kidney Beans (*Sookha Rajmah*)

SLOW COOKER SIZE: 3½ QUART (3.32 L); SOAKING TIME: 5 HOURS; COOKING TIME: 4½ HOURS ON LOW; YIELD: 8 CUPS (1.90 L)

3 cups (681 g) whole dried kidney beans, picked over and washed

6 cups (1.42 L) water, for soaking

5 cups (1.19 L) water, for cooking

1. Soak the beans in the 6 cups soaking water for 5 hours.

2. Drain. (Kidney beans do better if soaked before cooking.)

3. Put the beans in the slow cooker and add the 5 cups cooking water. (See page 47 for details on making this dish without a slow cooker.)

4. Cook on low for 4½ hours.

5. Rinse the beans in a colander with cold water to stop the cooking process and drain any excess liquid.

6. Store the beans in the refrigerator for up to 1 week or in the freezer up to 3 months.

To make this dish in a 5-quart (4.74-L) slow cooker, use 6 cups (1.36 kg) dried kidney beans, soak them in 12 cups water (2.84 L). Drain this water and cook them in 8 cups fresh water (1.90 L) on low for 4½ hours. A double recipe makes 14 cups (3.32 L).

Cooked, Plain Green Lentils (*Sookhi Sabut Moong Dal*)

SLOW COOKER SIZE: 3½ QUART (3.32 L); COOKING TIME: 2½ HOURS ON LOW; YIELD: 8 CUPS (1.90 L)

:::

3 cups (576 g) whole dried green lentils (*sabut moong dal*), picked over and washed

5 cups (1.19 L) water

1. Put the lentils and water in the slow cooker. Cook on low for 2½ hours. I found that the low heat worked better for lentils, which can dry up easily if cooked on high. (See page 47 for details on making this dish without a slow cooker.)

2. Rinse the beans in a colander with cold water to stop the cooking process and drain any excess liquid.

3. Store the lentils in the refrigerator for up to 1 week and in the freezer up to 3 months.

To make this dish in a 5-quart (4.74-L) slow cooker, use 6 cups (1.15 kg) dried green lentils and 8 cups (1.90 L) water. Cook on low for 2½ hours. A double recipe makes 14 cups (3.32 L).

Cooked, Plain Adzuki Beans

SLOW COOKER SIZE: 3½ QUART (3.32 L); COOKING TIME: 3½ HOURS ON LOW; YIELD: 8 CUPS (1.90 L)

:::

3 cups (591 g) whole dried adzuki beans, picked over and washed

5 cups (1.19 L) water

1. Put the beans and water in the slow cooker. (See page 47 for details on making this dish without a slow cooker.)

2. Cook on low for 3½ hours.

3. Rinse the beans in a colander with cold water to stop the cooking process and drain any excess liquid.

4. Store the beans in the refrigerator for up to 1 week and in the freezer up to 3 months.

To make this dish in a 5-quart (4.74-L) slow cooker, use 6 cups (1.18 kg) dried adzuki beans and 8 cups (1.90 L) water. Cook on low for 3½ hours. A double recipe makes 14 cups (3.32 L).

North Indian Hummus

YIELD: 2 CUPS (474 ML)

2 cups (396 g) cooked whole beans or lentils

Juice of 1 medium lemon

1 clove garlic, peeled, trimmed and coarsely chopped

1 teaspoon coarse sea salt

1 teaspoon ground black pepper

½ teaspoon Roasted Ground Cumin (see recipe on page 62)

½ teaspoon ground coriander

¼ cup (4 g) chopped fresh cilantro

⅓ cup (79 mL) plus 1 tablespoon olive oil

1–4 tablespoons (15–60 mL) water

½ teaspoon paprika, for garnish

1. In a food processor, combine the beans or lentils, lemon juice, garlic, salt, black pepper, cumin, coriander, and cilantro. Process until well mixed.

2. With the machine still running, add the oil. Continue to process until the mixture is creamy and smooth, adding water as needed, 1 tablespoon at a time.

3. Serve garnished with the paprika and with toasted *naan*, pita, or *papad* on the side.

Try This! Garnish your dip with anything from chopped red onions to a teaspoon of grated ginger root, or even some finely sliced green chiles.

South Indian Hummus

YIELD: 2 CUPS (474 ML)

2 cups (396 g) cooked whole beans or lentils

Juice of 1 lemon

1 clove garlic, peeled, trimmed and coarsely chopped

1 teaspoon coarse sea salt

1 teaspoon ground black pepper

½ teaspoon Roasted Ground Cumin (see recipe on page 62)

1 teaspoon *Rasam* Powder (see recipe on page 61) or *Sambhar Masala* (see recipe on page 60)

⅓ cup (79 mL) coconut oil

½ teaspoon asafetida (*hing*)

1 teaspoon black mustard seeds

1–4 tablespoons (15–60 mL) water

½ teaspoon paprika, for garnish

1. In a food processor, combine the beans or lentils, lemon juice, garlic, salt, black pepper, cumin, and *Rasam* Powder or *Sambhar Masala*.

2. In a sauté pan, heat the oil over medium-high heat.

3. Add the asafetida and mustard. Cook until the seeds start to sizzle and pop, about 30 seconds. Be careful, you might need to cover the pan.

4. Add the oil mixture to the food processor and blend until creamy and smooth, adding water as needed, 1 tablespoon at a time. Serve garnished with the paprika and with toasted *naan*, pita, or *papad* on the side.

Indian-Inspired Soup

YIELD: 6 CUPS (1.42 L)

Soup is one of my easiest go-to meals on busy school nights. For my girls, it's a treat in a bowl; for me, it's fast and easy but nutritious as well. Cook your main ingredient (whole beans or lentils) ahead of time, and a fantastic soup will be at your fingertips any day of the week.

1 teaspoon oil

1 medium yellow onion, peeled and diced (1 cup [150 g])

3 medium carrots, peeled, trimmed, and diced or cut into thin rounds (1 heaping cup [128 g])

3 celery stalks, trimmed and diced (1 heaping cup [120 g])

4 cloves garlic, peeled and grated or minced

1 tablespoon dried, split and skinned red lentils (*masoor dal*), picked over and washed

1½ teaspoons coarse sea salt

1 teaspoon ground cumin

½ teaspoon ground black pepper

6 cups (1.42 L) water

2 cups (396 g) cooked whole beans or lentils, or a mixture

1. In a soup pot, the heat oil over medium-high heat.

2. Add the onion, carrots, celery, and garlic.

3. Cook for 1 to 2 minutes, until the vegetables soften and the onion browns slightly.

4. Add the dried lentils, salt, cumin, pepper, and water and bring to a boil.

5. Reduce the heat and simmer uncovered for 20 minutes.

6. Add the cooked beans or lentils and heat through. Serve piping hot in bowls.

Try This! Get creative with the veggies—spinach, red and/or green bell pepper, and broccoli all work.

Roasted *Masala* Beans or Lentils

YIELD: 4 CUPS (948 ML)

This is another take on my Chickpea Poppers (see recipe on page 100). Obviously, chickpeas taste delicious prepped this way, but so do whole lentils, black-eyed peas, black chickpeas, adzuki beans...the list goes on and on.

4 cups (792 g) cooked whole beans or lentils

1 tablespoon *garam masala, Chaat Masala* **(see recipe on page 57) or** S*ambhar Masala* **(see recipe on page 60)**

2 teaspoons coarse sea salt

2 tablespoons oil

1 teaspoon red chile powder, cayenne, or paprika

1. Set an oven rack at the highest position. Preheat oven to 425°F (220°C). Line a baking sheet with aluminum foil for easy clean up.

2. In a large bowl, gently mix together the beans or lentils, *masala*, salt, and oil.

3. Arrange the seasoned beans or lentils in a single layer on the prepared baking sheet.

4. Bake for 15 minutes. Carefully take the tray out of oven, mix gently so that the beans or lentils cook evenly, and bake for another 10 minutes.

5. Cool for 15 minutes. Sprinkle with red chile, cayenne, or paprika. Serve immediately as a salad, over brown or white basmati rice, or stuffed in a *roti* wrap.

Warm North Indian Salad

YIELD: 3 CUPS (711 ML)

This is a terrific and quick warm salad that is downright addictive. I really like it with cooked adzuki beans, but just about any legume would work. It's so versatile that you can serve it over a bed of lettuce, over rice, with Indian bread, or stuffed in a pita.

1 tablespoon oil

1 teaspoon cumin seeds

½ teaspoon turmeric powder

1 medium yellow or red onion, peeled and chopped (1 cup [150 g])

1 (1-inch [2.5-cm]) piece ginger root, peeled and sliced into matchsticks

2 cloves garlic, peeled and grated

1–2 green Thai, serrano, or cayenne chiles, stems removed, chopped

2 cups (396 g) cooked whole beans or lentils

1 teaspoon coarse sea salt

½ teaspoon red chile powder or cayenne

½ teaspoon black salt (*kala namak*)

¼ cup (4 g) chopped fresh cilantro

1. In a deep, heavy pan, heat the oil over medium-high heat.

2. Add the cumin and turmeric. Cook until the seeds sizzle, about 30 seconds.

3. Add the onion, ginger root, garlic, and chiles. Cook until browned, about 2 minutes.

4. Add the beans or lentils. Cook another 2 minutes.

5. Add the sea salt, chile powder, black salt, and cilantro. Mix well and serve.

Try This! I love mixing in freshly sprouted lentils or beans toward the end. You don't want to kill the nutritional properties of the sprouts by cooking them, but adding them at the end will give you just enough flavor. We love eating the sprout concoction as a breakfast with a side of toast.

Cold North Indian Street Salad (*Chaat*)

YIELD: 6 CUPS (1.42 L)

Indian salads are so easy to make and so much fun to eat. Fresh cilantro and spices, rather than oil, provide flavor, making these salads some of the healthiest around. You can use any cooked beans or lentils, but one of my kids' favorites is brown whole lentils (masoor dal). Feel free to sub any veggies as well. I love grating in anything and everything, from beets, to carrots, to chopped cooked potatoes or even celery.

4 cups (792 g) cooked whole beans or lentils

1 medium red onion, peeled and diced (1 cup [150 g])

1 medium tomato, diced (1 cup [160 g])

1 small cucumber, peeled and diced (½ cup [65 g])

1 medium daikon, peeled and grated (1 cup [114 g])

1–2 green Thai, serrano, or cayenne chiles, stems removed, chopped

¼ cup (4 g) minced fresh cilantro, minced

Juice of 1 large lemon

1 teaspoon coarse sea salt

½ teaspoon black salt (*kala namak*)

½ teaspoon *Chaat Masala* (see recipe on page 57)

½ teaspoon red chile powder or cayenne

1 teaspoon fresh white turmeric, peeled and grated (optional)

1. In a deep bowl, mix together all the ingredients. Serve immediately as a side salad or wrapped in a lettuce leaf, or do as I do, and serve with a side of warm brown basmati rice as a quick meal.

Note: It's not easy to find fresh turmeric, let alone white turmeric, but if you happen to come across it, a little grated and sprinkled over the salad will provide taste and nutrition.

Quickie *Masala* Beans or Lentils

YIELD: 5 CUPS (1.19 L)

:::

1 cup (237 mL) *Gila Masala* (see recipe on page 63)

1 cup (150 g) chopped vegetables (squash, pumpkin, bell peppers, carrots, corn, cauliflower, or spinach)

1–3 Thai, serrano, or cayenne chiles, stems removed, chopped

1 teaspoon *garam masala*

1 teaspoon ground coriander

1 teaspoon Roasted Ground Cumin (see recipe on page 62)

½ teaspoon red chile powder or cayenne

1½ teaspoons coarse sea salt

2 cups (474 mL) water

2 cups (396 g) cooked whole beans or lentils

1 tablespoon chopped fresh cilantro, for garnish

1. In a deep, heavy saucepan, heat the *Gila Masala* over medium-high heat until it starts to bubble.

2. Add the vegetables, chiles, *garam masala*, coriander, cumin, red chile powder, salt, and water. Cook until the vegetables soften, 15 to 20 minutes.

3. Add the beans or lentils. Cook until warmed through.

4. Garnish with the cilantro and serve immediately with brown or white basmati rice, *roti*, or *naan*.

South Indian Legume Salad with Coconut

YIELD: 4 CUPS (948 ML)

:::

2 tablespoons coconut oil

½ teaspoon asafetida (*hing*)

1 teaspoon black mustard seeds

10–12 curry leaves, coarsely chopped

2 tablespoons unsweetened shredded coconut

4 cups (792 g) cooked whole beans or lentils

1 teaspoon coarse sea salt

1–2 Thai, serrano, or cayenne chiles, stems removed, sliced lengthwise

1. In a deep, heavy pan, heat the oil over medium-high heat.

2. Add the asafetida, mustard, curry leaves, and coconut. Heat until the seeds pop, about 30 seconds. Be careful not to burn the curry leaves or coconut. The seeds can pop out, so keep a lid handy.

3. Add the beans or lentils, salt, and chiles. Mix well and serve immediately.

Note: There is nothing better than freshly grated coconut, but if you cannot find it, use the dry, grated variety from the grocery store. Just make sure it is unsweetened.

North Indian Curried Beans or Lentils

YIELD: 5 CUPS (1.19 L)

2 tablespoons oil

½ teaspoon asafetida (*hing*)

2 teaspoons cumin seeds

½ teaspoon turmeric powder

1 (3-inch [7.5-cm]) cinnamon stick

1 cassia leaf (or bay leaf)

½ medium yellow or red onion, peeled and minced (½ cup [75 g])

1 (1-inch [2.5-cm]) piece ginger root, peeled and grated or minced

4 cloves garlic, peeled and grated or minced

2 large tomatoes, peeled and diced (2 cups [320 g])

2–4 green Thai, serrano, or cayenne chiles, stems removed, chopped

4 cups (792 g) cooked whole beans or lentils

4 cups (978 mL) water

1½ teaspoons coarse sea salt

1 teaspoon red chile powder or cayenne

2 tablespoons chopped fresh cilantro, for garnish

1. In a heavy saucepan, heat the oil over medium-high heat.

2. Add the asafetida, cumin, turmeric, cinnamon, and cassia leaf and cook until the seeds sizzle, about 30 seconds.

3. Add the onion and cook until slightly browned, about 3 minutes. Stir frequently so the onion doesn't stick to the pan.

4. Add the ginger root and garlic. Cook another 2 minutes.

5. Add the tomatoes and green chiles.

6. Reduce the heat to medium-low and cook for 3 to 5 minutes, until the tomatoes start to break down.

7. Add the beans or lentils and cook for another 2 minutes.

8. Add the water, salt, and red chile powder. Bring to a boil.

9. Once the mixture boiling, reduce the heat and simmer for 10 to 15 minutes.

10. Garnish with the cilantro and serve with brown or white basmati rice, *roti*, or *naan*.

Note: This recipe calls for just the right amount of water. If the legumes absorb some of the liquid and you want more curry, just add a little more water, and add a little more salt to taste.

South Indian Beans or Lentils with Curry Leaves

YIELD: 6 CUPS (1.42 L)

This was one of the most popular recipes in my last book—I still have people emailing me about it. Who would have thought such simple ingredients (curry leaves, coconut milk, and masoor dal*) could produce such magic? You can do the same with any legume. Just follow the recipe below, and you'll have the essence of South Indian cuisine and ingredients right at your fingertips, literally in minutes.*

2 tablespoons coconut oil

½ teaspoon asafetida powder (*hing*)

½ teaspoon turmeric powder

1 teaspoon cumin seeds

1 teaspoon black mustard seeds

15–20 fresh curry leaves, coarsely chopped

6 whole dried red chile peppers, coarsely chopped

½ medium yellow or red onion, peeled and diced (½ cup [75 g])

1 (14-oz. [420-mL]) can coconut milk, light or full fat

1 cup (237 mL) water

1 teaspoon *Rasam* Powder (see recipe on page 61) or *Sambhar Masala* (see recipe on page 60)

1½ teaspoons coarse sea salt

1 teaspoon red chile powder or cayenne

3 cups (576 g) cooked whole beans or lentils

1 tablespoon chopped fresh cilantro, for garnish

1. In a deep, heavy saucepan, heat the oil over medium-high heat.

2. Add the asafetida, turmeric, cumin, mustard, curry leaves, and red chile peppers. Cook until the seeds sizzle, about 30 seconds. Mustard seeds can pop, so keep a lid handy.

3. Add the onion. Cook until browned, about 2 minutes, stirring frequently to prevent sticking.

4. Add the coconut milk, water, *Rasam* Powder or *Sambhar Masala*, salt, and red chile powder. Bring to a boil, and then reduce the heat and simmer for 1 to 2 minutes, until the flavors infuse the milk.

5. Add the beans or lentils. Warm through and simmer for 2 to 4 minutes, until the legumes are infused with flavor. Add another cup of water if you want a soupier consistency. Serve immediately, garnished with the cilantro, in deep bowls with brown or white basmati rice.

Goan-Inspired Curry with Coconut Milk

YIELD: 6 CUPS (1.42 L)

The tastes of Goa are influenced by the state's coastal location and its history as a Portuguese colony. Seafood and coconut milk are commonly woven through the cuisine in this region. This curry is a fun, light dish that is a nice diversion from some of the fiery curries of North India. Feel free to experiment with any beans, but chickpeas and black-eyed peas work best.

1 tablespoon oil

½ large onion, peeled and diced (½ cup [75 g])

1 (1-inch [2.5-cm]) piece ginger root, peeled and grated or minced

4 cloves garlic, peeled and grated or minced

1 large tomato, diced (2 cups)

1–3 green Thai, serrano, or cayenne chiles, stems removed, chopped

1 tablespoon ground coriander

1 tablespoon ground cumin

1 teaspoon turmeric powder

1 teaspoon tamarind paste

1 heaping teaspoon jaggery (*gur*) or brown sugar

1½ teaspoons coarse sea salt

3 cups (711 mL) water

4 cups (792 g) cooked whole lentils or beans (black-eyed peas are traditional)

1 cup (237 mL) coconut milk, regular or light

Juice of ½ medium lemon

1 tablespoon chopped fresh cilantro, for garnish

1. In a deep, heavy saucepan, heat the oil over medium-high heat.

2. Add the onion and cook for 2 minutes, until slightly browned.

3. Add the ginger root and garlic. Cook another minute.

4. Add the tomato, chiles, coriander, cumin, turmeric, tamarind, jaggery, salt, and water.

5. Bring to a boil, reduce the heat, and simmer uncovered for 15 minutes.

6. Add the lentils or beans and coconut milk and heat through.

7. Add the lemon juice and garnish with the cilantro. Serve with brown or white basmati rice, *roti*, or *naan*.

Chana Masala Legumes

YIELD: 6 CUPS (1.42 L)

The spice chana masala *is used to make the dish* chana masala. *I know, a little confusing.* Chana *refers to white chickpeas, but this recipe is in this section to inspire you to take your spice blend and use it for any beans or lentils. The tanginess of this* masala *comes from dried pomegranate seeds and mango powder. It's absolutely delicious and, I warn you, highly addictive once you see how easy it is to whip up.*

2 tablespoons oil

1 heaping teaspoon cumin seeds

½ teaspoon turmeric powder

2 tablespoons *Chana Masala* (see recipe on page 58)

1 large yellow or red onion, peeled and diced (2 cups [300 g])

1 (2-inch [5-cm]) piece ginger root, peeled and grated or minced

4 cloves garlic, peeled and grated or minced

2 medium tomatoes, diced (2 cups [320 g])

1–3 green Thai, serrano, or cayenne chiles, stems removed, chopped

1 teaspoon red chile powder or cayenne

1 tablespoon coarse sea salt

1 cup (237 mL) water

4 cups (792 g) cooked whole beans or lentils (white chickpeas are traditional)

1. In a deep, heavy pan, heat the oil over medium-high heat.

2. Add the cumin, turmeric, and *Chana Masala* and cook until the seeds sizzle, about 30 seconds.

3. Add the onion and cook until soft, about a minute.

4. Add the ginger root and garlic. Cook another minute.

5. Add the tomatoes, green chiles, red chile powder, salt, and water.

6. Bring to a boil, reduce the heat, and simmer the mixture for 10 minutes, until all the ingredients blend together.

7. Add the beans or lentils and cook through. Serve over brown or white basmati rice or with *roti* or *naan*.

Punjabi Curried Beans (*Rajmah*-Inspired Curry)

YIELD: 7 CUPS (1.66 L)

1 medium yellow or red onion, peeled and roughly chopped (1 cup [150 g])

1 (2-inch [5-cm]) piece ginger root, peeled and roughly chopped

4 cloves garlic, peeled and trimmed

2–4 green Thai, serrano, or cayenne chiles, stems removed, chopped

2 tablespoons oil

½ teaspoon asafetida (*hing*)

2 teaspoons cumin seeds

1 teaspoon turmeric powder

1 (3-inch [7.5-cm]) cinnamon stick

2 whole cloves

1 black cardamom pod

2 medium tomatoes, peeled and diced (1 cup)

2 tablespoons tomato paste

4 cups (792 g) cooked whole beans or lentils (kidney beans are traditional)

2 cups (474 mL) water

2 teaspoons coarse sea salt

2 teaspoons *garam masala*

1 teaspoon red chile powder or cayenne

2 heaping tablespoons minced fresh cilantro

1. In a food processor, process the onion, ginger root, garlic, and chiles to a watery paste.

2. In a deep, heavy pan, heat the oil over medium-high heat.

3. Add the asafetida, cumin, turmeric, cinnamon, cloves, and cardamom. Cook until the mixture sizzles, about 30 seconds.

4. Slowly add the onion paste. Be careful—this can splatter when it hits the hot oil. Cook until browned, stirring occasionally, about 2 minutes.

5. Add the tomatoes, tomato paste, lentils or beans, water, salt, *garam masala*, and red chile powder.

6. Bring the mixture to a boil, then reduce the heat and simmer for 10 minutes.

7. Remove the whole spices. Add the cilantro and serve over a bed of brown or white basmati rice.

Stovetop *Sambhar*-Inspired Curry

YIELD: 9 CUPS (2.13 L)

2 cups (396 g) cooked whole beans or lentils

9 cups (2.13 L) water

1 medium potato (any kind), peeled and diced (about 2 cups [300 g])

1 teaspoon tamarind paste

5 cups (750 g) vegetables (use a variety), diced and julienned

2 heaping tablespoons *Sambhar Masala* (see recipe on page 60)

1 tablespoon oil

1 teaspoon asafetida powder (*hing*) (optional)

1 tablespoon black mustard seeds

5–8 whole dried red chiles, roughly chopped

8–10 fresh curry leaves, coarsely chopped

1 teaspoon red chile powder or cayenne

1 tablespoon coarse sea salt

1. In a deep soup pot over medium-high heat, combine the beans or lentils, water, potato, tamarind, vegetables, and *Sambhar Masala*. Bring to a boil.

2. Reduce the heat and simmer for 15 minutes, until the vegetables wilt and soften.

3. Prepare the tempering (*tarka*). In a small pan, heat the oil over medium-high heat. Add the asafetida (if using) and mustard seeds. Mustard tends to pop, so keep a lid handy.

4. Once the seeds start to pop, quickly add the red chiles and curry leaves. Cook for another 2 minutes, stirring frequently.

5. Once the curry leaves start to brown and curl up, add this mixture to the lentils. Cook for another 5 minutes.

6. Add the red chile powder and salt. Serve as a hearty soup, as a traditional side to *dosa*, or with brown or white basmati rice.

Slow-Cooked Beans and Lentils

Punjabi Curried Lima Beans

SLOW COOKER SIZE: 3½ QUART (3.32 L); COOKING TIME: 7 HOURS ON HIGH; YIELD: 10 CUPS (2.37 L)

I was never a fan of lima beans—until now. I was curious to try this recipe after my friend, professional chef Jill Houk, told me she had had lima beans on hand and subbed them for kidney beans in my Punjabi Red Beans (Rajmah) recipe from my last book. After tweaking the spices a bit, this dish was born. I could eat it every night. Even my husband has become a fan of lima beans. Thanks, Jill!

2 cups (454 g) dried lima beans, picked over and washed

½ medium yellow or red onion, peeled and roughly chopped (½ cup [75 g])

1 medium tomato, diced (1 cup [160 g])

1 (1-inch [2.5-cm]) piece of ginger root, peeled and grated or minced

2 cloves garlic, peeled and grated or minced

1–3 green Thai, serrano, or cayenne chiles, stems removed, chopped

3 whole cloves

1 heaping teaspoon cumin seeds

1 teaspoon red chile powder or cayenne

1 heaping teaspoon coarse sea salt

½ teaspoon turmeric powder

½ teaspoon *garam masala*

7 cups (1.66 L) water

¼ cup (4 g) chopped fresh cilantro

1. Put all the ingredients except the cilantro in the slow cooker. Cook on high for 7 hours, until the beans break down and become somewhat creamy. About halfway through the cooking process, the beans will look like they are finished, but keep the slow cooker going. The curry will still be watery and will need to cook down further. (See page 47 for details on making this dish without a slow cooker.)

2. Remove the cloves if you can find them. Add the fresh cilantro and serve over basmati rice or with *roti* or *naan*.

To make this dish in a 5-quart (4.74-L) slow cooker, double all ingredients except water (use 10 cups [2.37 L] water). Cook on high for 7 hours. A double recipe makes 14 cups (3.32 L).

Five Lentil Stew (*Panchratna Dal*)

SLOW COOKER SIZE: 3½ QUART (3.32 L); COOKING TIME: 6 HOURS ON HIGH; YIELD: 10 CUPS (2.37 L)

A popular dish in the northwest Indian state of Rajasthan, panchratna dal is as wholesome as it is delicious. It's a combination of five lentils, four of them in their healthiest form—whole rather than split. I like making this with a tiny bit less water than my other lentil preparations, so that it has the consistency of a hearty stew or chili. Serve it up Indian style or sprinkle a little grated cheese over it and put it out over a bed of tortilla chips.

½ cup (96 g) dried whole black lentils with skin (*sabut urad*), picked over and washed

½ cup (96 g) dried whole green lentils with skin (*sabut moong*), picked over and washed

½ cup (96 g) dried whole brown lentils (*sabut massoor*), picked over and washed

½ cup (96 g) dried whole pigeon peas (*sabut toor*), picked over and washed

½ cup (96 g) split gram (*chana dal*), picked over and washed

½ medium yellow or red onion, peeled and roughly chopped (½ cup [75 g])

½ medium tomato, peeled and halved

1 (1-inch [2.5-cm]) piece of ginger root, peeled and cut into pieces

2 cloves garlic, peeled and trimmed

1–3 green Thai, serrano, or cayenne chiles, stems removed, chopped

½ cup (8 g) fresh cilantro

1 whole clove

1 green cardamom pod, lightly crushed

1 black cardamom pod

1 (2-inch [5-cm]) cinnamon stick

2 teaspoons cumin seeds, divided

1 teaspoon coarse sea salt

1 teaspoon ground coriander

1 teaspoon turmeric powder

1 teaspoon red chile powder or cayenne

7 cups (1.66 L) water

1 tablespoon oil

1. Put the lentils (black, green, brown, pigeon peas, and split gram) in the slow cooker. (See page 47 for details on making this dish without a slow cooker.)

2. In a food processor, process the onion, tomato, ginger root, garlic, chiles, and cilantro until smooth.

3. Add this mixture to the slow cooker.

4. Add the clove, green and black cardamom pods, cinnamon, 1 teaspoon of the cumin, salt, coriander, turmeric, red chile powder, and water to the slow cooker.

5. Cook on high for 6 hours.

6. In a sauté pan, heat the oil over medium-high heat. Add the remaining 1 teaspoon cumin and cook until the seeds sizzle. Drizzle this over the lentil dish and mix it in. Remove the whole spices. Serve topped with chopped fresh cilantro, onions, and green chiles, along with brown or white basmati rice, *roti*, or *naan*.

Try This! Feel free to substitute any lentils for those listed. If you only have a few varieties, just increase the amount you use so that the total amount is the same. As long as the recipe balances the quantity of lentils to the amount of water you use, it will turn out great.

To make this dish in a 5-quart (4.74-L) slow cooker, double all ingredients except water and cinnamon stick (use 10 cups [2.37 L] water and only 1 [2-inch][5-cm] cinnamon stick). Cook on high for 7 hours. A double recipe makes 13 cups (3.08 L).

Chana and Split *Moong Dal* with Pepper Flakes

SLOW COOKER SIZE: 3½ QUART (3.32 L); COOKING TIME: 5 HOURS ON HIGH; YIELD: 8 CUPS (1.90 L)

I love the combination of these two lentils. Cooked together, they not only complement one another in taste, they also become incredibly creamy. The pepper flakes add just enough pizazz that you'll be left wanting more than one bowl!

1 cup (192 g) split gram (*chana dal*), picked over and washed

1 cup (192 g) dried split green lentils with skin (*moong dal*), picked over and washed

½ medium yellow or red onion, peeled and diced (½ cup [75 g])

1 (1-inch [2.5-cm]) piece ginger root, peeled and grated or minced

4 cloves garlic, peeled and grated or minced

1 medium tomato, peeled and diced (1 cup [160 g])

1–3 green Thai, serrano, or cayenne chiles, stems removed, chopped

1 tablespoon plus 1 teaspoon cumin seeds, divided

1 teaspoon turmeric powder

2 teaspoons coarse sea salt

1 teaspoon red chile powder or cayenne

6 cups (1.42 L) water

2 tablespoons oil

1 teaspoon red pepper flakes

2 tablespoons minced fresh cilantro

1. Put the split gram, green lentils, onion, ginger root, garlic, tomato, chiles, 1 tablespoon of the cumin, turmeric, salt, red chile powder, and water in the slow cooker. Cook on high for 5 hours. (See page 47 for details on making this dish without a slow cooker.)

2. Near the end of the cooking time, heat the oil in a shallow pan over medium-high heat.

3. Add the remaining 1 teaspoon of cumin.

4. Once it is sizzling, add the red pepper flakes. Cook for another 30 seconds at the most. If you cook it too long, the flakes will get too hard.

5. Add this mixture, along with the cilantro, to the lentils.

6. Serve this alone as a soup or with brown or white basmati rice, *roti*, or naan.

To make this dish in a 5-quart (4.74-L) slow cooker, double all ingredients except water (use 10 cups [2.37 L] water). Cook on high for 6 hours. A double recipe makes 15 cups (3.55 L).

Vegetables

Ginger Soy Milk Soup (*Adarak ki Sabji*)

YIELD: 3½ CUPS (3.32 L)

As the story goes, my paternal grandfather's younger brother went on a religious retreat in the hills and came back with this recipe—a ginger-based masala mixed with milk. Ever since, our family has been among the only ones in our village of Bhikhi with the recipe to this amazing, yet very simple, soup. Typically, it's made in the winter and served with thick roti. *Though I grew up eating it with dairy milk, my mother made it with soy milk once, and even my dad had to admit it tasted better.*

2 cups plain unsweetened soy milk

¼ cup (59 mL) *Adarak Masala* **(see recipe on page 64)**

½ teaspoon coarse sea salt

½ teaspoon red chile powder or cayenne

1–3 green Thai, serrano, or cayenne chiles, stems removed, chopped

½ cup (119 mL) water (optional)

¼ cup (4 g) chopped, fresh cilantro

1. In a pot over medium-high heat, bring the soy milk to a light boil.

2. Add the *Adarak Masala*, salt, red chile powder, green chiles, and water (if using). Bring to a boil, add cilantro, and serve with thick *roti* or *naan*.

Spiced Tofu, Bell Pepper, and Tomatoes

YIELD: 4 CUPS (948 ML)

I love making this dish in a flash when I've got no grand plan for dinner. It's easy, it's healthy, and I usually have all the ingredients on hand. It's a delicious solution to getting dinner on the table fast.

2 tablespoons oil

1 heaping tablespoon cumin seeds

1 teaspoon turmeric powder

1 medium red or yellow onion, peeled and minced (1 cup [150 g])

1 (2-inch [5-cm]) piece ginger root, peeled and grated or minced

6 cloves garlic, peeled and grated or minced

2 medium tomatoes, peeled (optional) and chopped (3 cups [480 g])

2–4 green Thai, serrano, or cayenne chiles, stems removed, chopped

1 tablespoon tomato paste

1 tablespoon *garam masala*

1 tablespoon dried fenugreek leaves (*kasoori methi*), lightly crushed by hand to release their flavor

1 cup (237 mL) water

2 teaspoons coarse sea salt

1 teaspoon red chile powder or cayenne

2 medium green bell peppers, seeded and diced (2 cups)

2 (14-ounce [397-g]) packages extra-firm organic tofu, baked and cubed (see the Baked, Spiced Tofu recipe on page 68)

1. In a large, heavy pan, heat the oil over medium-high heat.

2. Add the cumin and turmeric. Cook until the seeds sizzle, about 30 seconds.

3. Add the onion, ginger root, and garlic. Cook for 2 to 3 minutes, until lightly browned, stirring occasionally.

4. Add the tomatoes, chiles, tomato paste, *garam masala*, fenugreek, water, salt, and red chile powder. Reduce the heat slightly and simmer uncovered for 8 minutes.

5. Add the bell peppers and cook for another 2 minutes. Add the tofu and mix gently. Cook for another 2 minutes, until heated through. Serve with brown or white basmati rice, *roti*, or *naan*.

Spiced Peas and "Paneer" (Mattar "Paneer")

YIELD: 7 CUPS (1.66 L)

My mother and mother-in-law both make a great mattar paneer. In fact, theirs are so good that I'd rather not disappoint my husband with my own version when it comes to his favorite dish. With this recipe, I finally got close enough to the experts in my family. Even with the tofu substitution, it's delicious—baking the tofu first makes all the difference in the world.

2 tablespoons oil

1 heaping teaspoon cumin seeds

1 teaspoon turmeric powder

1 (2-inch [5-cm]) cinnamon stick

1 black cardamom pod

1 large yellow or red onion, peeled and minced (2 cups [300 g])

1 (2-inch [5-cm]) piece ginger root, peeled and grated or minced

6–8 cloves garlic, peeled and grated or minced

2 medium tomatoes, peeled and diced (3 cups [480 g])

3 tablespoons (45 mL) tomato paste

2–4 green Thai, serrano, or cayenne chiles, stems removed, chopped

3 cups (711 mL) water, divided

1 heaping teaspoon *garam masala*

1 heaping teaspoon ground coriander

1 teaspoon red chile powder or cayenne

2 teaspoons coarse sea salt

1 pound (454 g) fresh or 1 (16-ounce [454-g]) bag frozen peas

1 (14-ounce [397-g]) package extra-firm organic tofu, baked and cubed (see the Baked, Spiced Tofu recipe on page 68)

2 tablespoons chopped fresh cilantro, for garnish

1. In a large, heavy pan, heat the oil over medium-high heat.

2. Add the cumin, turmeric, cinnamon, and cardamom and cook until the seeds sizzle, about 30 seconds.

3. Add the onion and cook until browned, about 3 minutes, stirring occasionally.

4. Add the ginger root and garlic. Cook for another minute, stirring to avoid sticking.

5. Add the tomatoes, tomato paste, chiles, 1 cup of the water, *garam masala*, coriander, red chile powder, and salt and bring to a boil. Reduce the heat and simmer uncovered for 10 minutes.

6. Remove and discard the cinnamon stick and cardamom. Blend the mixture, either using an immersion blender or by transferring it to a blender or food processor. (This step is not necessary, but it adds smoothness to your final dish.)

7. Add the peas, baked tofu cubes, and remaining 2 cups (474 mL) water. Bring to a boil, reduce to a simmer, and cook for 10 minutes, uncovered.

8. Garnish with the cilantro. Serve with brown or white basmati rice, *roti*, or *naan*.

Cumin Potato Hash (*Jeera Aloo*)

YIELD: 4 CUPS (948 ML)

This is such a fun recipe for weekend mornings when you want to switch up your regular hash browns. The cumin is warm and inviting and pairs perfectly with the potatoes. Boil the potatoes the night before to get these on the breakfast table nice and fast.

1 tablespoon oil

1 tablespoon cumin seeds

½ teaspoon asafetida (*hing*)

½ teaspoon turmeric powder

½ teaspoon mango powder (*amchur*)

1 small yellow or red onion, peeled and diced (1 cup [150 g])

1 (1-inch [2.5-cm]) piece ginger root, peeled and grated or minced

3 large boiled potatoes (any kind), peeled and diced (4 cups [600 g])

1 teaspoon coarse sea salt

1–2 green Thai, serrano, or cayenne chiles, stems removed, thinly sliced

¼ cup (4 g) minced fresh cilantro, minced

Juice of ½ lemon

1. In a deep, heavy pan, heat the oil over medium-high heat.

2. Add the cumin, asafetida, turmeric, and mango powder. Cook until the seeds sizzle, about 30 seconds.

3. Add the onion and ginger root. Cook for another minute, stirring to prevent sticking.

4. Add the potatoes and salt. Mix well and cook until the potatoes are warmed through.

5. Top with the chiles, cilantro, and lemon juice. Serve as a side with *roti* or *naan* or rolled in a *besan poora* or *dosa*. This is great as a filling for a veggie sandwich or even served in a lettuce cup.

Mustard Seed Potato Hash

YIELD: 4 CUPS (948 ML)

I love finding ways to throw lentils into my dishes. They add a subtle crunch and texture that can't be beat, especially here when you pair them with potatoes.

1 tablespoon split gram (*chana dal*)

1 tablespoon oil

1 teaspoon turmeric powder

1 teaspoon black mustard seeds

10 curry leaves, roughly chopped

1 small yellow or red onion, peeled and diced (1 cup [150 g])

3 large boiled potatoes (any kind), peeled and diced (4 cups [600 g])

1 teaspoon coarse white salt

1–2 green Thai, serrano, or cayenne chiles, stems removed, sliced thin

1. Soak the split gram in boiled water while you prep the remaining ingredients.

2. In a deep, heavy pan, heat the oil over medium-high heat.

3. Add the turmeric, mustard, curry leaves, and drained split gram. Be careful, the seeds tend to pop and the soaked lentils might splash oil, so you may need a lid. Cook for 30 seconds, stirring to prevent sticking.

4. Add the onion. Cook until slightly browned, about 2 minutes.

5. Add the potatoes, salt, and chiles. Cook for another 2 minutes. Serve as a side with *roti* or *naan* or rolled in a *besan poora* or *dosa*. This is great as a filling for a veggie sandwich or even served in a lettuce cup.

Chickpea Flour Curry with Veggies (Punjabi Khardi)

YIELD: 8 CUPS (1.90 L)

Making this dish with soy yogurt seemed impossible. I was desperate to try it, because it's one of my favorite meals—especially for lunch on the weekend. Every family has its own version of this dish. It took me a couple of tries, but I finally did it! I absolutely love this recipe and I make it over and over now for my family.

2 cups (474 mL) plain, unsweetened soy yogurt

¼ cup (23 g) gram (chickpea) flour (*besan*)

4 cups (978 mL) water

1 tablespoon turmeric powder

2 tablespoons oil

1 teaspoon mango powder (*amchur*)

½ teaspoon fenugreek seeds

1 (4-inch [10-cm]) piece ginger root, peeled and grated

6 cloves garlic, peeled and grated or minced

6 cups (900 g) mixed vegetables (such as carrots, cauliflower, eggplant, cabbage, and red onion), diced

1–4 green Thai, serrano, or cayenne chiles, stems removed, chopped

1 teaspoon red chile powder or cayenne

1 tablespoon plus 1 teaspoon coarse sea salt

½ teaspoon ground black pepper

6 whole dried red chiles, coarsely chopped

2 tablespoons chopped fresh cilantro, for garnish

1 small handful spinach, chopped, for garnish

1. Put the yogurt, gram flour, water, and turmeric in a blender and process well. The result will look like a frothy yellow milkshake.

2. In a heavy, deep saucepan, heat the oil over medium-high heat.

3. Add the mango powder and fenugreek. Heat until the seeds just start to brown. Do not let them overcook, as they will become bitter.

4. Add the ginger root and garlic. Cook for 2 minutes, until browned, stirring occasionally to prevent sticking.

5. Add the vegetables, green chiles, red chile powder, salt, and black pepper. Cook until the vegetables are just wilted, about 4 minutes, stirring occasionally.

6. Add the yogurt mixture and dried red chiles and bring to a boil. Reduce the heat to medium-low and simmer uncovered for at least 20 minutes.

7. Garnish with the cilantro and spinach. Serve over brown or white basmati rice.

Slow-Cooker Spiced Peas and "*Paneer*"

SLOW COOKER SIZE: 3½ QUART (3.32 L); COOKING TIME: 3 HOURS ON HIGH; YIELD: 7 CUPS (1.66 L)

About six months after my first book, The Indian Slow Cooker, *was released, I got a frantic phone call from my father. He was up in arms after realizing that a recipe for* mattar paneer, *my husband's favorite dish, was not included. I told him I didn't bother toying with it, thinking it couldn't be done. I mean, how would peas taste in the slow cooker? My mom tackled the recipe to prove me wrong and to help ensure that her favorite son-in-law gets his go-to dish whenever he wants. The credit for this recipe goes entirely to my mother—oh, and I guess my father, too, for noting the discrepancy!*

1 large yellow or red onion, peeled and roughly chopped (2 cups [300 g])

1 (2-inch [5-cm]) piece ginger root, peeled and roughly chopped

6–8 cloves garlic, peeled and trimmed

1 (16-ounce) bag frozen peas

3 medium tomatoes, peeled and chopped (4 cups [640 g])

2–3 green Thai, serrano, or cayenne chiles, stems removed, chopped

1 black cardamom pod

1 (2-inch [5-cm]) cinnamon stick

1 tablespoon cumin seeds

1 teaspoon *garam masala*

1 teaspoon ground coriander

1 teaspoon red chile powder or cayenne

2 teaspoons coarse sea salt

2 heaping tablespoons tomato paste

3½ cups (830 mL) boiling water

1 (14-ounce [397-g]) package extra-firm organic tofu, baked and cubed (see the Baked, Spiced Tofu recipe on page 68)

2 tablespoons chopped fresh cilantro, for garnish

1. In a food processor, process the onion, ginger root, and garlic into a paste. Put this mixture in the slow cooker. (See page 47 for details on making this dish without a slow cooker.)

2. Add the peas, tomatoes, chiles, cardamom, cinnamon, cumin, *garam masala*, coriander, red chile powder, salt, and tomato paste.

3. Pour the boiling water slowly over all the ingredients. Mix gently.

4. Cook on high for 2½ hours. Add the tofu and cook for another 30 minutes.

5. Garnish with the cilantro and serve with brown or white basmati rice, *roti*, or *naan*.

Note: Chopped tomatoes, boiling water, and baked tofu are essential to getting this recipe right. Trust me. I tried to grind the tomatoes and use unboiled water and unbaked tofu. The dish was a disaster!

To make this dish in a 5-quart (4.74-L) slow cooker, double all the ingredients. Cook on high for a total of 4 hours, following the steps above. A double recipe makes 14 cups (3.32 L).

Punjabi-Style Cabbage (*Band Gobi*)

SLOW COOKER SIZE: 3½ QUART (3.32 L),
COOKING TIME: 4 HOURS ON LOW; YIELD: 7 CUPS (1.66 L)

One of the first times I made this dish for my kids, they went crazy stuffing it in a roti *like a taco. This is a delicious, easy recipe that will make cooking dinner fun. The dish is traditionally made on the stovetop, but it comes out great in a slow cooker as well.*

3 tablespoons (45 mL) oil

1 tablespoon cumin seeds

1 teaspoon turmeric powder

½ yellow or red onion, peeled and diced (½ cup [75 g])

1 (1-inch [2.5-cm]) piece ginger root, peeled and grated or minced

6 cloves garlic, peeled and minced

1 medium potato, peeled and diced (1 cup [150 g])

1 medium head white cabbage, outer leaves removed and finely shredded (about 8 cups [560 g])

1 cup (145 g) peas, fresh or frozen

1 green Thai, serrano, or cayenne chile, stem removed, chopped

1 teaspoon ground coriander

1 teaspoon ground cumin

1 teaspoon ground black pepper

½ teaspoon red chile powder or cayenne

1½ teaspoons sea salt

SLOW COOKER INSTRUCTIONS:

1. Put all the ingredients in the slow cooker and mix gently.

2. Cook on low for 4 hours. Serve with white or brown basmati rice, *roti*, or *naan*. This is a great filler for a pita with a little drizzle of soy yogurt *raita*.

STOVETOP INSTRUCTIONS:

1. In a deep, heavy pan, heat the oil over medium-high heat. Add the cumin and turmeric and cook until the seeds sizzle, about 30 seconds.

2. Add the onion, ginger root, and garlic and cook for 2 minutes, stirring occasionally to prevent sticking.

3. Add the potato. Cook for 2 minutes, until soft.

4. Add the cabbage and cook for another 3 to 4 minutes, stirring occasionally to make sure all of the cabbage is mixed well with the spices.

5. Add the peas, chile, coriander, cumin, black pepper, red chile powder, and salt.

6. Turn the heat to low and partially cover the pan. Cook until the cabbage wilts, about 8 to 10 minutes. Some like to cook it a little longer. My kids like it a tiny bit crunchy.

Cabbage with Mustard Seeds and Coconut

YIELD: 6 CUPS (1.42 L)

I love, love, love cabbage made this way. It's such an easy vegetable to cook and with the simple ingredients I've presented below, you'll take your cabbage to new flavor heights. You'll love the subtle addition of protein with the soaked lentils.

2 tablespoons whole, skinned black lentils (*sabut urud dal*)

2 tablespoons coconut oil

½ teaspoon asafetida (*hing*)

1 teaspoon black mustard seeds

10–12 curry leaves, coarsely chopped

2 tablespoons unsweetened shredded coconut

1 medium head white cabbage, chopped (8 cups [560 g])

1 teaspoon coarse sea salt

1–2 Thai, serrano, or cayenne chiles, stems removed, sliced lengthwise

1. Soak the lentils in boiled water so they soften while you prep the remaining ingredients.

2. In a deep, heavy pan, heat the oil over medium-high heat.

3. Add the asafetida, mustard, drained lentils, curry leaves, and coconut. Heat until the seeds pop, about 30 seconds. Be careful not to burn the curry leaves or coconut. The seeds can pop out, so keep a lid handy.

4. Add the cabbage and salt. Cook, stirring regularly, for 2 minutes until the cabbage just wilts.

5. Add the chiles. Serve immediately as a warm salad, cold, or with *roti* or *naan*.

Note: There is nothing better than freshly grated coconut, but if you cannot find it, use the dry, grated variety from the grocery store. Just make sure it is unsweetened.

String Beans with Potatoes

YIELD: 5 CUPS (1.19 L)

We grew up eating this dish once a week. It's a pretty popular Punjabi dish and tastes even better the next day with leftover rotis *for lunch!*

1 tablespoon oil

1 teaspoon cumin seeds

½ teaspoon turmeric powder

1 medium red or yellow onion, peeled and diced (1 cup [150 g])

1 (1-inch [2.5-cm]) piece ginger root, peeled and grated or minced

3 cloves garlic, peeled and grated or minced

1 medium potato, peeled and diced (1 cup [150 g])

¼ cup (59 mL) water

4 cups (680 g) chopped string beans (½-inch [13-mm] long)

1–2 Thai, serrano, or cayenne chiles, stems removed, chopped

1 teaspoon coarse sea salt

1 teaspoon red chile powder or cayenne

1. In a heavy, deep pan, heat the oil over medium-high heat.

2. Add the cumin and turmeric, and cook until the seeds sizzle, about 30 seconds.

3. Add the onion, ginger root, and garlic. Cook until slightly brown, about 2 minutes.

4. Add the potato and cook for another 2 minutes, stirring constantly. Add the water to prevent sticking.

5. Add the string beans. Cook for 2 minutes, stirring occasionally.

6. Add the chiles, salt, and red chile powder.

7. Reduce the heat to medium-low and partially cover the pan. Cook for 15 minutes, until the beans and potato are soft. Turn off the heat and let the pan sit, covered, on the same burner for another 5 to 10 minutes.

8. Serve with white or brown basmati rice, *roti,* or *naan.* You can also do as I do and stuff this inside a pita topped with chopped onions and tomatoes for a quickie low-cal lunch.

Babaji's Eggplant with Potatoes

YIELD: 6 CUPS (1.42 L)

This is the very first dish I learned how to cook when I was just 10 years old. It was my paternal grandfather, Babaji, who gave me my first cooking lesson one rainy Saturday afternoon when he and my grandmother were visiting from their village in the heart of Punjab, India. I'll never forget how he stopped me from throwing away the green, woody stem of the eggplant, saying that it holds the tastiest meat of the vegetable. To this day, I cook eggplant with the woody stem, and I was amazed when at one meal my 6-year-old, un-prompted, took a stem and sucked out the center, just like Babaji had showed me.

2 tablespoons oil

½ teaspoon asafetida (*hing*)

1 teaspoon cumin seeds

½ teaspoon turmeric powder

1 (2-inch [5-cm]) piece ginger root, peeled and cut into ½-inch (13-mm) long matchsticks

4 cloves garlic, peeled and roughly chopped

1 medium potato, peeled and roughly chopped (2 cups [300 g])

1 large onion, peeled and roughly chopped (2 cups [300 g])

1–3 Thai, serrano, or cayenne chiles, stems removed, chopped

1 large tomato, roughly chopped (2 cups [320 g])

4 medium eggplants with skin, roughly chopped, woody ends included (8 cups [656 g])

2 teaspoons coarse sea salt

1 tablespoon *garam masala*

1 tablespoon ground coriander

1 teaspoon red chile powder or cayenne

2 tablespoons chopped fresh cilantro, for garnish

1. In a deep, heavy pan, heat the oil over medium-high heat.

2. Add the asafetida, cumin, and turmeric. Cook until the seeds sizzle, about 30 seconds.

3. Add the ginger root and garlic. Cook, stirring constantly, for 1 minute.

4. Add the potato. Cook for 2 minutes.

5. Add the onions and chiles and cook for another 2 minutes, until slightly brown.

6. Add the tomato and cook for 2 minutes. At this point, you'll have created a base for your dish.

7. Add the eggplant. (It's important to keep the woody ends so that you and your guests can chew out the delicious, meaty center later.)

8. Add the salt, *garam masala*, coriander, and red chile powder. Cook for 2 minutes.

9. Turn the heat to low, partially cover the pan, and cook for another 10 minutes.

10. Turn the heat off, cover the pan completely, and let it sit for 5 minutes so that all the flavors have a chance to really blend. Garnish with the cilantro and serve with *roti* or *naan*.

Masala Brussels Sprouts

YIELD: 4 CUPS (948 ML)

Brussels sprouts are not commonly found on the Indian dinner table, but we love them in our house. I had a bag in my fridge from my weekly organic veggie delivery from my favorite Chicago home-delivery service, Irv and Shelly's Fresh Picks. I decided to try making a curry out of them and was pleasantly surprised. They not only held up in terms of texture, they were amazingly delicious—my kids literally gobbled them up.

1 tablespoon oil

1 teaspoon cumin seeds

2 cups (474 mL) *Gila Masala* (see recipe on page 63)

1 cup (237 mL) water

4 tablespoons (60 mL) Cashew Cream (see recipe on page 65)

4 cups (352 g) Brussels sprouts, trimmed and halved

1–3 Thai, serrano, or cayenne chiles, stems removed, chopped

2 teaspoons coarse sea salt

1 teaspoon *garam masala*

1 teaspoon ground coriander

1 teaspoon red chile powder or cayenne

2 tablespoons chopped fresh cilantro, for garnish

1. In a deep, heavy pan, heat the oil over medium-high heat.

2. Add the cumin and cook until the seeds sizzle, about 30 seconds.

3. Add the North Indian Tomato Soup Stock, water, Cashew Cream, Brussels sprouts, chiles, salt, *garam masala*, coriander, and red chile powder.

4. Bring to a boil. Reduce the heat and simmer uncovered for 10 to 12 minutes, until the Brussels sprouts soften.

5. Garnish with the cilantro and serve over brown or white basmati rice or with *roti* or *naan*.

Beets with Mustard Seeds and Coconut

YIELD: 3 CUPS (711 ML)

The weekend before I planned to hand in the manuscript for this book, I attended a party thrown by my good friends and fellow foodies Minu and Jesse Benawra. One of their childhood friends, Vid, mentioned the one dish he knows how to make: South Indian-inspired beets. My interest was immediately piqued as I listened to him describe the dish his mother, Sharada Byanna, taught him how to make. I really wanted to include beets in this book because I love them, but I had never had them prepared in an Indian way that worked for me. This one is it.

1 tablespoon oil

1 teaspoon black mustard seeds

1 medium yellow or red onion, peeled and diced (1½ cups [225 g])

2 teaspoons ground cumin

2 teaspoons ground coriander

1 teaspoon South Indian *masala* (*sambhar*, *rasam*, or chutney powders)

1 tablespoon unsweetened, shredded coconut

5–6 small beets, peeled and diced (3 cups [408 g])

1 teaspoon coarse sea salt

1½ [356 mL] cups water

1. In a heavy pan, heat the oil over medium-high heat.

2. Add the mustard seeds and cook until they sizzle, about 30 seconds.

3. Add the onion and cook until slightly brown, about 1 minute.

4. Add the cumin, coriander, South Indian *masala*, and coconut. Cook for 1 minute.

5. Add the beets and cook for 1 minute.

6. Add the salt and water. Bring to a boil, reduce the heat, cover, and simmer for 15 minutes.

7. Turn the heat off and let the pan sit, covered, for 5 minutes so the dish can absorb all the flavors. Serve over brown or white basmati rice or with *roti* or *naan*.

Grated *Masala* Squash

YIELD: 4 CUPS (948 ML)

My mother's youngest sister sent me this recipe by email from her home in Chandigarh. I love it because it's such a simple way to use up the squash that normally pile up in my house from weeks of fall organic shipments. Grating squash makes cooking it so much easier, and the absence of chiles and heat make this a perfect, healthy go-to dish for my kids.

2 tablespoons oil

2 teaspoons cumin seeds

2 teaspoons ground coriander

1 teaspoon turmeric powder

1 large squash or pumpkin (any kind of winter or summer squash will work), peeled and grated (8 cups [928 g])

1 (2-inch [5-cm]) piece ginger root, peeled and cut in matchsticks (⅓ cup [32 g])

1 teaspoon coarse sea salt

2 tablespoons water

Juice of 1 lemon

2 tablespoons chopped fresh cilantro

1. In a deep, heavy pan, heat the oil over medium-high heat.

2. Add the cumin, coriander, and turmeric. Cook until the seeds sizzle, about 30 seconds.

3. Add the squash, ginger root, salt, and water. Cook for 2 minutes and mix well.

4. Cover the pan and reduce the heat to medium low. Cook for 8 minutes.

5. Add the lemon juice and cilantro. Serve with *roti* or *naan*, or do as I do, and serve on a toasted English muffin topped with thinly sliced rings of yellow or red onion.

Note: If you are making this for your kids, you might want to grate the ginger root instead of leaving it as matchsticks.

Try This! Mix and match with this recipe. Grate and add whatever squash or pumpkin you like. Indian pumpkin is squat and green on the outside and orange on the inside. I've only found it in Indian grocery stores. It's absolutely delicious, but you'll get a very similar dish with anything from butternut to acorn squash. I have even successfully used standard pumpkins left over from Halloween decorations for this dish (only if the pumpkins have not been carved).

Cashew-Stuffed Baby Eggplant

YIELD: 20 BABY EGGPLANTS

For my wedding in 1999, my mother hired an older Gujarati woman to do all the cooking for the week-long festivities. She made a stuffed eggplant dish that even had my husband, who has never been a fan of this vegetable, asking for more. Though the original recipe calls for peanuts, I prefer cashews, which taste smoother and richer. Either way, this will be a dish you'll make again and again. It's truly delicious and incredibly easy.

½ cup (69 g) raw cashews

20 baby eggplants

2 tablespoons oil, divided

1 teaspoon cumin seeds

1 teaspoon coriander seeds

1 tablespoon sesame seeds

½ teaspoon black mustard seeds

½ teaspoon fennel seeds

¼ teaspoon fenugreek seeds

1 large yellow or red onion, peeled and diced (2 cups [300 g])

1 (1-inch [2.5-cm]) piece ginger root, peeled and grated or minced

4 cloves garlic, peeled and roughly chopped

1–3 Thai, serrano, or cayenne chiles, stems removed, chopped

1 teaspoon turmeric powder

1 teaspoon grated jaggery (*gur*)

2 teaspoons *garam masala*

1 tablespoon coarse sea salt

1 teaspoon red chile powder or cayenne

1 cup (237 mL) water, divided

2 tablespoons chopped fresh cilantro, for garnish

1. Soak the cashews in water while you prep the remaining ingredients.

2. Cut 2 perpendicular slits in each eggplant from the bottom, working toward the stem and stopping before you cut through the eggplant. They should stay intact. You'll have 4 sections when done, held together by the green, woody stem. Place them in a bowl of water while you prep the remaining ingredients. This will help open up the eggplants slightly so that you can better stuff them later.

3. In a heavy pan, heat 1 tablespoon of the oil over medium-high heat.

4. Add the cumin, coriander, sesame, mustard, fennel, and fenugreek seeds. Cook until the seeds pop slightly, about 30 seconds. Don't overcook this—the fenugreek can get bitter.

5. Add the onion, ginger root, garlic, and chiles. Cook until the onion is browned, about 2 minutes.

6. Add the turmeric, jaggery, *garam masala*, salt, red chile powder, and drained cashews. Cook for another 2 minutes, until well blended.

7. Transfer this mixture to a food processor. Add ½ cup (119 mL) of the water and process until smooth. Take your time; you may need to stop and scrape down the sides.

8. The eggplants are now ready to be stuffed! Holding an eggplant in one hand, put about 1 tablespoon of the mixture in the core of the eggplant, covering all sides.

9. Gently close the eggplant back up and place it in a large bowl until you finish stuffing all the eggplants.

10. In a large, deep pan, heat the remaining 1 tablespoon oil over medium-high heat. Add the eggplants gently, one at a time. Add the leftover *masala* and the remaining ½ cup water and reduce the heat to medium-low. Cover the pan and cook for 20 minutes, gently stirring occasionally, being careful to keep the eggplants intact.

11. Turn off the heat and let the eggplants sit for 5 minutes to really cook through and absorb all the flavors. Garnish with the cilantro and serve over rice or with *roti* or *naan*.

Note: Using fresh eggplant is key in this recipe, because small eggplants that have been sitting around tend to get rubbery skins. If the skin is a little tough, it will likely start to pull away during the cooking process. Simply remove and discard that excess skin. The flesh inside will still be moist and delicious.

Spiced Spinach with "*Paneer*" (Palak "*Paneer*")

YIELD: 10 CUPS (2.37 L)

This is probably one of the most commonly known Indian dishes in the West—and one of the most seemingly complicated. In fact, it is utterly simple to make. I like having a large batch on hand because we eat through it so quickly. This is one of my girls' favorite dishes—and I never even have to hide the spinach.

2 tablespoons oil

1 tablespoon cumin seeds

1 teaspoon turmeric powder

1 large yellow or red onion, peeled and diced (2 cups [300 g])

1 (2-inch [5-cm]) piece ginger root, peeled and grated or minced

6 cloves garlic, peeled and grated or minced

2 large tomatoes, chopped (2 cups [320 g])

1–2 Thai, serrano, or cayenne chiles, stems removed, chopped

2 tablespoons tomato paste

1 cup (237 mL) water

1 tablespoon ground coriander

1 tablespoon *garam masala*

2 teaspoons coarse sea salt

12 cups (360 g) densely packed chopped fresh spinach

1 (14-ounce [397-g]) package extra-firm, organic tofu, baked and cubed (see the Baked, Spiced Tofu recipe on page 68)

1. In a wide, heavy pan, heat the oil over medium-high heat.

2. Add the cumin and turmeric and cook until the seeds sizzle, about 30 seconds.

3. Add the onion and cook until brown, about 3 minutes, stirring gently so it doesn't stick.

4. Add the ginger root and garlic. Cook for 2 minutes.

5. Add the tomatoes, chiles, tomato paste, water, coriander, *garam masala*, and salt. Reduce the heat and simmer for 5 minutes.

6. Add the spinach. You might need to do this in batches, adding more as it wilts. It will look like you have way too much spinach, but not to worry. It will all cook down. Trust me!

7. Cook for 7 minutes, until the spinach is wilted and cooked down. Blend with an immersion blender or in a traditional blender. If you don't like it puréed (as it's traditionally eaten), skip this step.

8. Add the tofu and cook for another 2 to 3 minutes. Serve with *roti* or *naan*.

Curried Winter Melon (*Ghiya ki Sabji*)

YIELD: 3 CUPS (711 ML)

My mom used to make this simple and homey take on winter melon on the weekends for a quick lunch. I still love it served simply over a bed of basmati rice. Although it's not a commonly found vegetable, most ethnic grocery stores carry it.

2 tablespoons oil

½ teaspoon asafetida (*hing*)

1 teaspoon cumin seeds

½ teaspoon turmeric powder

1 medium winter melon, skin left on, diced (6 cups [696 g])

1 medium tomato, diced (1 cup [160 g])

1. In a deep, heavy pan, heat the oil over medium-high heat.

2. Add the asafetida, cumin, and turmeric and cook until the seeds sizzle, about 30 seconds.

3. Add the winter melon. Cook for 3 minutes, until the melon softens.

4. Add the tomato, reduce the heat to low, and partially cover the pan. Cook for 15 minutes.

5. Turn off the heat. Adjust the lid so it covers the pan completely, and let the pan sit for 10 minutes to completely combine flavors. Serve with brown or white basmati rice and a side of soy yogurt *raita*.

Fenugreek–Spinach Potatoes (Methi-Palak Aloo)

YIELD: 3 CUPS (711 ML)

My mother's dear friend Kamlesh Bhatia gave my mom this recipe. It's as delicious as she promised.

2 tablespoons oil

1 teaspoon cumin seeds

1 (12-ounce [341-g]) package frozen spinach

1½ cups (42 g) dried fenugreek leaves (*kasoori methi*), crushed lightly in one hand to release their flavor

1 large potato, peeled and diced (2 cups [300 g])

1 teaspoon coarse sea salt

½ teaspoon turmeric powder

¼ teaspoon red chile powder or cayenne

¼ cup (59 mL) water

1. In a heavy pan, heat the oil over medium-high heat.

2. Add the cumin and cook until the seeds sizzle, about 30 seconds.

3. Add the spinach and reduce the heat to medium-low. Cover the pan and cook for 5 minutes.

4. Add the fenugreek leaves, mix gently, replace the lid, and cook for another 5 minutes.

5. Add the potato, salt, turmeric, red chile powder, and water. Mix gently.

6. Replace the lid and cook for 10 minutes.

7. Take the pan off the heat and let it sit with the lid on for another 5 minutes. Serve with *roti* or *naan*.

Crackling Okra (*Bhindi Masala*)

YIELD: 4 CUPS (948 ML)

The first vegetable I remember eating and loving is, of all things, okra. I still remember picking it from my grandmother's backyard in Chandigarh. It was fresh, crisp, and delicious. And, made Punjabi-style, it is completely addictive. Even my husband agrees that my recipe is one of the best he's ever tasted.

2 tablespoons oil

1 teaspoon cumin seeds

1 teaspoon turmeric powder

1 large yellow or red onion, peeled and very roughly chopped (2 cups [300 g])

1 (1-inch [2.5-cm]) piece ginger root, peeled and grated or minced

3 garlic cloves, peeled and chopped, minced, or grated

2 pounds (908 g) okra, washed, dried, trimmed and cut into ¼-inch (6-mm) rounds (6 cups)

1–2 Thai, serrano, or cayenne chiles, stems removed, chopped

½ teaspoon mango powder (*amchur*)

1 teaspoon red chile powder or cayenne

1 teaspoon *garam masala*

2 teaspoons coarse sea salt

1 tablespoon chopped fresh cilantro, for garnish

1. In a deep, heavy pan, heat the oil over medium-high heat.

2. Add the cumin and turmeric. Cook until the seeds start to sizzle, about 30 seconds.

3. Add the onion and cook until browned, 2 to 3 minutes. This is a key step for my okra. The large, chunky pieces of onion should brown all over and slightly caramelize. This will be a delicious base for the final dish.

4. Add the ginger root and garlic. Cook for 1 minute, stirring occasionally.

5. Add the okra and cook for 2 minutes, just until the okra turns bright green and starts to get a tiny bit lacy. Don't worry—we're going to get rid of the laciness!

6. Add the chiles, mango powder, red chile powder, *garam masala*, and salt. Cook for 2 minutes, stirring occasionally.

7. Reduce the heat to low and partially cover the pan. Cook for 7 minutes, stirring occasionally.

8. Turn off the heat and adjust the lid so it covers the pot entirely. Let it sit for 3 to 5 minutes to allow all the flavors to be absorbed.

9. Garnish with the cilantro and serve with brown or white basmati rice, *roti*, or *naan*.

Note: Many people dislike okra because of its laciness. My *Suraj Massi* (maternal aunt) taught me to use the mango powder to get rid of that stringy lace for which okra is typically known.

The key to making this dish successfully is in drying the okra completely after washing it—and before cutting it.

Bell Peppers and Potato

YIELD: 3 CUPS (711 ML)

There is something warm and inviting about pairing these two ingredients with cumin. I love the combination and like to keep this dish on hand to eat as a go-to snack or quickie lunch with leftover rotis.

2 tablespoons oil

1 teaspoon cumin seeds

½ teaspoon asafetida (*hing*)

½ teaspoon turmeric powder

4 cloves garlic, peeled and chopped

1 large yellow or red onion, peeled and roughly chopped (2 cups [300 g])

1 large potato, peeled and diced (1½ cups [225 g])

½ teaspoon mango powder (*amchur*)

½ teaspoon *garam masala*

½ teaspoon ground coriander

2 teaspoons coarse sea salt

3 large green bell peppers, cleaned and diced (4 cups [600 g])

1. In a heavy pan, heat the oil over medium-high heat.

2. Add the cumin and cook until the seeds sizzle, about 30 seconds.

3. Add the asafetida, turmeric, and garlic. Cook until the garlic is slightly browned, about 30 seconds.

4. Add the onion and cook for about 1 minute, until it is slightly browned.

5. Add the potato, mango powder, *garam masala*, coriander, and salt. Cook until the potato is softened, about 3 minutes.

6. Add the peppers and cook for another 3 minutes.

7. Reduce the heat to low, partially cover the pan, and cook for another 3 minutes.

8. Turn off the heat, adjust the lid so it completely covers the pan, and let the dish sit for 10 minutes to let the flavors blend. Serve with *roti* or *naan*.

String Beans with Toasted *Chana Dal*

YIELD: 3 CUPS (711 G)

My mom started making this dish a few years ago, and I just had to get the recipe. With the addition of lentils, it's very South Indian-inspired, and it's a wonderful way to get a little added protein with your veggies.

1 tablespoon oil

1 teaspoon cumin seeds

1 tablespoon split gram (*chana dal*), soaked in hot water

4 cups (about 1½ pounds [680 g]) green string beans, cut into ½-inch (13-mm) pieces

1 medium yellow or red onion, peeled and roughly chopped (2 cups [300 g])

2 green Thai, serrano, or cayenne chiles, stems removed, chopped

1 teaspoon mango powder (*amchur*)

½ teaspoon turmeric powder

1 teaspoon coarse sea salt

½ teaspoon red chile powder or cayenne

¼ cup (59 mL) water

1. In a heavy, deep pan, heat the oil over medium-high heat.

2. Add the cumin and cook until the seeds sizzle, about 30 seconds.

3. Add the drained split gram. The idea is to cook the dal, but not burn it. Cook, stirring occasionally, for 2 minutes.

4. Add the string beans, onion, chiles, mango powder, turmeric, salt, red chile powder, and water. Cook, stirring occasionally, for another 2 minutes. Reduce the heat to medium-low and partially cover the pan. Cook for about 10 minutes, stirring occasionally.

5. At this point the beans should be soft and the split gram should be cooked but still a tiny bit crunchy. Adjust the lid to cover the pan completely, turn off the heat, and allow the flavors to meld together for about 5 minutes.

6. Serve hot with a side of brown or white basmati rice, stuffed in a pita, or on top of a steaming hot *roti* or *naan*. I personally love a bowl simply topped with chopped fresh onions.

Sweet and Sour Sweet Potatoes

YIELD: 4 CUPS (948 ML)

This dish is traditionally made with an Indian-style pumpkin that is green on the outside and slightly orange on the inside. It's absolutely delicious. Sweet potatoes have a similar texture and taste. Substitute winter squash or pumpkin for the sweet potato and it will be just as delicious—all at once sweet, sour, and spicy.

2 tablespoons oil

½ teaspoon fenugreek seeds

1 large sweet potato, peeled and cubed (4 cups [600 g])

1–3 Thai, serrano, or cayenne chiles, stems removed, chopped

1 teaspoon coarse sea salt

½ teaspoon red chile powder or cayenne

1 heaping tablespoon jaggery (*gur*) or brown sugar

Juice of ½ lemon

1 tablespoon chopped fresh cilantro

1. In a wide, heavy pan, heat the oil over medium-high heat.

2. Add the fenugreek and cook until the seeds just start to sizzle and turn light brown. Don't overcook them, or they will turn bitter.

3. Add the sweet potato and chiles and cook for 3 minutes, until lightly browned, stirring occasionally to prevent sticking. (I like to blacken them slightly. It adds to the flavor.)

4. Reduce the heat to low and partially cover the pan. Cook for 3 to 4 more minutes.

5. Turn off the heat. Add the salt, red chile powder, jaggery, lemon juice, and cilantro. Replace the lid, covering the pan completely, and allow the dish to sit for 5 minutes. Serve with *naan* or *roti*, as a filler in my Chickpea Flour Crêpes (see recipe on page 79 and photo at right), or in a *dosa*.

Sneh Massi's Ripe Banana Curry (Pakka Kela ki Sabji)

YIELD: 2 CUPS (474 ML)

The story goes that my mother's eldest sister watched her mother-in-law cook this dish. She was immediately impressed by how easy it was to create a dish that's simply comfort in a bowl—at once sweet and spicy. I added heat with the chiles, but the recipe—straight from Delhi—is how my Massi makes it to this day.

1 tablespoon oil

1 teaspoon cumin seeds

1 small onion, peeled and diced (¾ cup [113 g])

1 medium tomato, peeled and diced (1½ cups [240 g])

1–3 green Thai, serrano, or cayenne chiles, thinly sliced

½ teaspoon coarse sea salt

4 ripe bananas, peeled and cut in ¼-inch (6-mm) rounds (3 cups [450 g])

1. In a deep, heavy pan, heat the oil over medium-high heat.

2. Add the cumin and cook until the seeds sizzle, about 30 seconds.

3. Add the tomato, chiles, and salt. Turn the heat to medium-low and cover the pan. Cook for 2 to 3 minutes, until the tomato softens into a slight sauce.

4. Add the bananas. Replace the lid and simmer for 15 minutes. Serve over a bed of brown or white basmati rice.

Spicy Plantains

YIELD: 2½ CUPS (593 ML)

Though they are not a commonly eaten vegetable in North India, plantains are delicious when prepped this way. My mom and I came up with the recipe while experimenting one night. She'd eaten it at a friend's house, and our attempt to replicate that recipe turned out pretty well.

2 large green plantains, unpeeled, cut in 2-inch (5-cm) long pieces

2 tablespoons oil

1 teaspoon cumin seeds

1 teaspoon black mustard seeds

1 medium onion, peeled and diced (1 cup [150 g])

1–2 green Thai, serrano, or cayenne chiles, chopped

½ teaspoon turmeric powder

1 teaspoon coarse sea salt

½ teaspoon red chile powder or cayenne

1 cup (237 mL) water

1. In a saucepan, bring water to a boil. Add the plantains. Reduce the heat to low and simmer for 15 minutes. Remove the plantains from the water remove their skins, and let cool. Once they are cool, dice them.

2. In a heavy pan, heat the oil over medium-high heat.

3. Add the cumin and mustard seeds and cook until they sizzle, about 30 seconds.

4. Add the onion. Cook until browned, about 2 minutes, stirring occasionally.

5. Add the plantains, chiles, turmeric, salt, red chile powder, and water.

6. Reduce the heat to low, partially cover the pan, and let the mixture simmer for 10 minutes, stirring occasionally.

7. Remove the pan from the heat, adjust the lid so it completely covers the pan, and let the mixture sit for another 5 minutes to let all the flavors blend.

8. Serve with brown or white basmati rice, *roti*, or *naan*.

South Indian Stew

YIELD: 9 CUPS (2.13 L)

Sambhar is the spicy and fragrant soup served along with dosas in South India. On a recent trip to South India, I found that most of the chefs I met were amazed when I told them that I make it frequently. First of all, it's delicious, and second, it helps me clear out my vegetable drawer. The sambhar masala used is key.

- 1 cup (192 g) split and skinned pigeon peas (*dhuli toor dal*)
- 11 cups (2.61 L) boiled water, divided
- 1 medium potato (any kind), peeled and diced (about 2 cups [300 g])
- 1 (1-inch [2.5-cm]) lump of tamarind pulp or 1 teaspoon tamarind paste
- 1 cup (237 mL) water
- 5 cups (750 g) vegetables (see step 3), diced and julienned
- 2 heaping tablespoons *Sambhar Masala* (see recipe on page 60)
- 1 tablespoon oil
- 1 teaspoon asafetida powder (*hing*) (optional)
- 1 tablespoon black mustard seeds
- 5–8 whole dried red chiles, roughly chopped
- 8–10 fresh curry leaves, coarsely chopped
- 1 teaspoon red chile powder or cayenne
- 3 teaspoons coarse sea salt

1. Soak the pigeon peas in 2 cups (474 mL) of the boiled water for 20 minutes until they soften slightly. Drain, discard the water, and transfer the lentils to a large saucepan. Add the potato and the remaining boiled water. Simmer on medium to medium-high heat for 40 minutes. At this point, the dal will be soft and broken down.

2. While the dal cooks, put the tamarind in a small pan with 1 cup (237 mL) water. Bring to a boil and simmer for about 15 minutes, until the tamarind breaks down. If the water starts to evaporate too much, add a little more. Press against the pulp with the back of a spoon and remove any seeds. Set the tamarind juice mixture aside. If you are using tamarind paste, just whirl it in about 1 cup of boiled water until it dissolves.

3. Prep the vegetables. I kept it flexible here, because just about any type of vegetables will do. The heartier root vegetables are best. Some suggestions: carrots, zucchini, cauliflower, daikon, white cabbage, onion, broccoli, kale, mushrooms, sweet potatoes, bell peppers, parsnips, and turnips. I love mixing up the cuts as well—I dice some veggies and julienne others.

4. Add the vegetables to the dal mixture and cook for another 20 minutes.

5. Add the tamarind juice mixture from Step 2 and the *sambhar* powder. Cook for another 10 minutes.

6. Prepare the tempering (*tarka*). In a small pan, heat the oil over medium-high heat. Add the asafetida (if using) and mustard seeds. Cover the pan so the seeds don't pop out and burn you. Once they start to pop, quickly add the red chiles and curry leaves. Cook for another 2 minutes, stirring frequently. Once the curry leaves start to brown and curl up, add this mixture to the lentils.

7. Mix in the red chile powder and salt. Serve as a hearty soup or as a traditional side to *dosa*.

Note: It's important to add the tamarind toward the end. Adding it too early will prevent the dal and vegetables from cooking and breaking down. You can try this dish with other yellow, quick-cooking *dals*, including *dhuli moong* and split and skinned *masoor*; just reduce the cooking time a bit.

Mushroom and Pea Sabji
(Mushroom aur Mattar ki Sabji)

YIELD: 3 CUPS (711 ML)

If you love mushrooms like I do, this is the dish for you. It's a standard in most North Indian households. The mushrooms and peas are beautifully pulled together with the spices to create a well-balanced dish that seems complicated but is actually quick to make.

1 tablespoon oil

1 teaspoon cumin seeds

½ teaspoon turmeric powder

½ teaspoon *garam masala*

2 cloves garlic, peeled and grated or minced

1 small yellow or red onion, peeled and minced (1 cup [150 g])

1 cup (145 g) peas, fresh or frozen

6 cups (450 g) mushrooms, washed, trimmed, and halved or quartered

½ teaspoon red chile powder or cayenne

1 teaspoon coarse sea salt

1. In a deep, heavy pan, heat the oil over medium-high heat.

2. Add the cumin, turmeric, and *garam masala*. Cook until the seeds sizzle, about 30 seconds.

3. Add the garlic. Cook for about 30 seconds, until the garlic is slightly browned.

4. Add the onion. Cook for 1 to 2 minutes, until browned.

5. Add the peas. Cook for 1 to 2 minutes, stirring to avoid sticking.

6. Add the mushrooms, red chile powder, and salt. Reduce the heat to medium-low and cook for 5 minutes, until the juices released from the mushrooms evaporates slightly.

7. Serve with brown or white basmati rice, *roti*, or *naan*.

Mushrooms in Cashew Cream Sauce

YIELD: 5 CUPS (1.19 L)

This was the very first recipe I wrote and tested for this cookbook. I was in heaven using Cashew Cream as a substitute for regular cream. I served it at a dinner party, and my good friend Karen Lurie not only liked it—she had no idea it was vegan. You'll fool your dinner guests too.

6 tablespoons (90 mL) Cashew Cream (see recipe on page 65)

½ cup (119 mL) water

1 teaspoon coarse sea salt

2 tablespoons oil

4 green cardamom pods, slightly crushed

2 black cardamom pods

1 (2-inch [5-cm]) cinnamon stick

4 whole cloves

2 cassia leaves (or bay leaves)

1 small yellow or red onion, peeled and minced (½ cup [75 g])

2 cloves garlic, peeled and grated or minced

2–3 pounds (.908–1.36 kg) small cremini mushrooms, cleaned and trimmed (8 cups [1.9 L])

½ teaspoon red chile powder or cayenne

1 tablespoon chopped fresh cilantro or parsley, for garnish

1. Mix together the Cashew Cream, water, and salt. Set aside.

2. In a deep, heavy pan, heat the oil over medium-high heat.

3. Add the green and black cardamom, cinnamon, cloves, and cassia leaves. Cook for 1 to 2 minutes, until aromatic.

4. Add the onion and garlic. Cook until brown, 2 to 4 minutes.

5. Add the mushrooms and cook for 6 minutes, until they soften, stirring occasionally to avoid sticking.

6. Make a well in the middle of the mixture. Add the Cashew Cream mixture and heat through, 2 to 3 minutes.

7. Remove the whole spices. Add the red chile powder and garnish with the fresh cilantro or parsley. Serve immediately with brown or white basmati rice.

Note: Small, whole mushrooms work best in this curry. If you can't find small mushrooms, just buy the bigger ones and slice them in half. I opt for cremini here because they add much more flavor than white button mushrooms.

Rice Dishes and One-Pot Meals

Cumin Rice (Jeera Chawal)

YIELD: 9 CUPS (2.13 L)

Few food smells bring back as many childhood memories as jeera chawal. *It was always the last thing my mother cooked before a big party. The warm smell of cumin and other spices sizzling with fresh onions in hot oil has always stayed with me and represented comfort, good food, and home. I couldn't care less what people say about white rice and carbs. I love my* jeera chawal!

1 tablespoon oil

1 heaping teaspoon cumin seeds

4 whole cloves

2 black cardamom pods

1 (3-inch [7.5-cm]) cinnamon stick

½ large yellow onion, peeled and thinly sliced (1 cup [150 g])

2 cups (380 g) uncooked white basmati rice, washed

½ teaspoon coarse sea salt

4 cups (978 mL) water

1. In a heavy, deep, wide pan, heat the oil over medium-high heat.

2. Add the cumin, cloves, cardamom, and cinnamon and cook until the seeds sizzle, about 30 seconds.

3. Add the onion. Cook until browned, stirring occasionally, about 2 minutes.

4. Add the rice and salt. Sauté for about 1 minute, stirring gently to ensure the rice does not stick.

5. Add the water and bring to a boil. Reduce the heat to low, partially cover the pan, and simmer until the moisture evaporates (about 8 minutes).

6. Turn off the heat and let the rice sit, completely covered, for 15 minutes. (I find that this step really helps evaporate any remaining moisture and produces tastier rice.) Remove and discard the whole spices. Fluff with a fork before serving.

Fennel Brown Rice (*Saunf Chawal*)

YIELD: 7 CUPS (1.66 L)

Brown rice has come a long way! It used to be shunned by most South Asians for being too hard and dense. Even my dad spent years fighting my mom's attempts to get him to eat brown rice. These days, there are more varieties to choose from, including long-grain basmati versions. I suggest trying it again and subbing it for white rice at times to get all the nutritional benefits of the whole grain. If you don't want to make the switch right away, mix in cooked brown rice with your favorite cooked white rice and transition slowly.

1 tablespoon oil

1 teaspoon cumin seeds

1 teaspoon fennel seeds

4 green cardamom pods, slightly crushed

2 black cardamom pods

4 whole cloves

1 (3-inch [7.5-cm]) cinnamon stick

2 cups (380 g) brown basmati rice, washed

½ teaspoon coarse sea salt

4 cups (978 mL) water

1. In a heavy, wide pan, heat the oil over medium-high heat.

2. Add the cumin, fennel, green and black cardamom, cloves, and cinnamon. Heat the spices until fragrant, about 1 to 2 minutes.

3. Add the rice and salt. Cook for 2 minutes, stirring a few times to prevent the rice from sticking.

4. Add the water and bring to a boil. Reduce the heat to low, partially cover the pan, and simmer for 20 to 25 minutes. Once the rice is cooked, turn off the heat, cover the pot completely, and let it sit for another 10 minutes. Fluff with a fork, remove the whole spices, and serve immediately.

Spiced Veggie Brown Rice (*Pulao*)

YIELD: 10 CUPS (2.37 L)

Years ago in Luton, England, my mother's brother, Yog Mamaji, had a group of the family visiting from the United States and India over for brunch. In no time, he and my cousin Alka whipped up a delicately spiced rice pulao *with simple frozen vegetables and served with a side of yogurt* raita. *It was as quick and easy as it was wholesome and delicious. I always remember this family moment when I sit down to a bowl of rice* pulao.

1 tablespoon oil

2 teaspoons cumin seeds

½ teaspoon turmeric powder

2 cups (150 g) frozen mixed cut vegetables (carrots, corn, string beans)

1 cup (138 g) raw cashews, roughly chopped

⅓ cup (55 g) golden raisins (optional)

2 cups (380 g) uncooked brown basmati rice

1 teaspoon coarse sea salt

5 cups (1.19 L) water

1. In a large, heavy pan, heat the oil over medium-high heat.

2. Add the cumin and turmeric. Cook until the seeds sizzle, about 30 seconds.

3. Add the vegetables (use fresh if frozen are not available), cashews, and raisins. Cook for 2 minutes, stirring frequently.

4. Add the rice and salt. Cook for another 2 minutes, stirring frequently.

5. Add the water and bring to a boil.

6. Reduce the heat to low, partially cover the pan, and simmer for 25 minutes. Turn off the heat, adjust the lid to completely cover the pan, and let the rice sit for 5 more minutes. Fluff and serve immediately with a side of soy yogurt *raita*.

Note: To make this dish with white basmati rice, use 4 cups (978 mL) water and reduce the cooking time to about 15 minutes. Some folks (including my kids) don't like raisins in their *pulao*. Whether to add them is your choice.

Lemon Brown Rice

YIELD: 6 CUPS (1.42 L)

The first time I had this dish was in the home of two of my close friends from South India, Padma and her younger sister Kshema. I still remember how my tongue and lips burned. I'd never eaten anything that spicy before. But I couldn't stop eating it, either. It was delicious. Most lemon rice dishes are made with white basmati rice, but I've swapped that out for brown rice and even for quinoa. The result was just as good as the original recipe.

¼ heaping cup (48 g) split gram (*chana dal*), picked over and washed

Juice of 4 small lemons

2 teaspoons turmeric powder

2 teaspoons coarse sea salt

1 heaping teaspoon chutney powder

2 tablespoons oil

½ teaspoon asafetida powder (*hing*)

4 whole dried red chile peppers, broken into pieces

10 fresh curry leaves, roughly chopped

1 tablespoon black mustard seeds

½ teaspoon coriander seeds, slightly crushed

2–4 green Thai, serrano, or cayenne chiles, sliced lengthwise

1 teaspoon peeled grated ginger root

½ cup water, or as needed

6 cups (1.14 kg) cooked brown basmati rice

¼ cup (40 g) unsalted raw peanuts, dry roasted

2 tablespoons fresh cilantro, minced

1. Soak the split gram in boiled water while you prep the remaining ingredients.

2. In a bowl, whisk together the lemon juice, turmeric, salt, and chutney powder. Set aside.

3. In a deep, heavy pan, heat the oil over medium-high heat.

4. Add the asafetida, dried red chiles, and curry leaves. Cook, stirring constantly, until the leaves curl slightly, about 1 minute.

5. Add the mustard and coriander seeds. Cook until they pop, about another minute.

6. Add the drained split gram. Cook for about 1 minute, until the lentils are lightly toasted.

7. Add the lemon juice mixture, green chiles, ginger root, and water. Heat to a gentle simmer, about 1 to 2 minutes.

8. Add the rice slowly and mix well.

9. Add the peanuts and cilantro. Serve as a one-pot meal with a side of coconut chutney or soy yogurt *raita*.

Tamarind Brown Rice

YIELD: 5 CUPS (1.19 L)

I always get my fix of tamarind rice at the temple. An auspicious dish, it is made and served on special and religious occasions in South India. Typically, the dish is made with white basmati rice. I wanted to show everyone how delicious it can be made with wholesome brown. Make it once this way, and you'll make it again…and again…and again.

1 heaping tablespoon split gram (*chana dal*), picked over and washed

2 tablespoons coconut oil

½ teaspoon asafetida powder (*hing*)

1 teaspoon ground fenugreek

1 teaspoon turmeric powder

1 teaspoon black mustard seeds

10–12 curry leaves, roughly chopped

6–8 dried red chile peppers, broken into pieces

1 heaping tablespoon raw peanuts, dry roasted

1 teaspoon coarse sea salt

1 teaspoon chutney powder

¾ cup (178 mL) Tamarind Juice (see recipe on page 66)

4 cups (760 g) cooked brown basmati rice

1. Soak the split gram in boiled water while you prep the remaining ingredients.

2. In a deep, heavy pan, heat the oil over medium-high heat.

3. Add the asafetida, fenugreek, turmeric, drained split gram, and mustard seeds. Cook until the seeds start sizzling, about 30 seconds. Mustard seeds tend to pop, so keep a lid handy. (The water from the drained split gram could also cause the oil to splash—be careful.)

4. Add the curry leaves, dried red chiles, peanuts, salt, and chutney powder. Cook for 30 seconds.

5. Add the Tamarind Juice and bring to a boil. Turn the heat to low and cook until the juice starts to thicken, about 3 minutes.

6. Add the rice and mix in slowly and completely.

7. Serve immediately as a stand-alone meal, as a quickie lunch, or with a side curry.

Note: Tamarind Juice gives this dish a more balanced flavor. If you don't have time to make the juice, just mix 1 teaspoon tamarind paste with ¾ cup water. If you don't have ground fenugreek powder, just grind the seeds in a spice grinder. You can also use a mortar and pestle, but you'll have to be patient. The seeds are hard and take time to break down by hand. If you don't have chutney powder on hand, just substitute another spice blend. You could even try curry powder.

Rice and Lentil Porridge (Healing *Kitchari*)

YIELD: 7 CUPS (1.66 L)

Kitchari to a Punjabi Indian is like chicken noodle soup to an American. It's at once healing and healthy, given to anyone with a stomachache. This recipe is the simplest stovetop recipe that I use for days when the kids are sick and just can't digest anything more complex.

1 cup (192 g) dried split and skinned green lentils (*dhuli moong dal*), picked over and washed

1 cup (174 g) white basmati rice, washed

6 cups (1.42 g) water

1 tablespoon oil

½ teaspoon asafetida (*hing*)

1 teaspoon cumin seeds

1 teaspoon carom seeds (*ajwain*)

½ teaspoon turmeric powder

1 tablespoon chopped yellow or red onion

1 teaspoon grated or minced ginger root

1½ teaspoons coarse sea salt

1. In a deep, heavy pot over medium-high heat, bring the lentils, rice, and water to a boil.

2. Reduce the heat to low and simmer for 17 minutes.

3. In a separate, shallow pan, heat the oil over medium-high heat.

4. Add the asafetida, cumin, carom, and turmeric. Cook until the seeds sizzle, about 30 seconds.

5. Add the onion and ginger root and cook until slightly brown, about 1 minute.

6. Add this mixture, along with the salt, to the lentil and rice mixture. Mix well and serve immediately with a dollop of soy butter and a side of Indian pickle (*achaar*). You can also top this with chopped onion and tomatoes.

Note: Because this dish is a combination of lentils and rice, it can get thick when it cools. The best way to reheat it is to add a little water to a serving in a pot and simmer it over medium-low heat until warmed through. Because you've added water, you might need to compensate for any lost flavor with a little more salt.

Split Gram and Brown Rice Porridge (*Chana Dal Kitchari*)

SLOW COOKER SIZE: 3½ QUART (3.32 L); COOKING TIME: 4 HOURS ON HIGH, YIELD: 7 CUPS (1.66 L)

My daughters have grown up on kitchari, *which in Hindi literally means "all mixed up." You take an equal portion of lentils and rice, mix them with simple spices, and you've got a meal that will amaze you. Just about any mix of lentils and rice will do the trick. During one of our visits to her home in King of Prussia, Pennsylvania, my mother used split gram with brown rice, and I just could not get enough of it. Neither could my kids.*

1 cup (192 g) split gram (*chana dal*), picked over and washed

1 cup (190 g) brown basmati rice, washed

½ medium yellow or red onion, peeled and minced (½ cup [75 g])

1 (½-inch [13-mm]) piece ginger root, peeled and grated or minced

2 garlic cloves, peeled and grated or minced

1–2 green Thai, serrano, or cayenne chiles, stems removed, chopped

2 teaspoons cumin seeds

2 teaspoons coarse sea salt

1 teaspoon turmeric powder

½ teaspoon red chile powder or cayenne

1 black cardamom pod

6 cups (1.42 L) water

1 tablespoon oil

1 teaspoon carom seeds (*ajwain*)

1. Put all the ingredients except the oil and carom seeds in the slow cooker. Cook on high for 4 hours. (See page 47 for details on making this dish without a slow cooker.)

2. When the 4 hours are up, make the tempering (*tarka*). In a small pan, heat the oil over medium-high heat.

3. Add the carom seeds. Once they begin to sizzle and brown slightly, after about 30 seconds, drizzle them over the *kitchari* in the slow cooker. Serve in a bowl topped with a dollop of Indian pickle (*achaar*) and chopped onions.

Note: Because this dish is a combination of lentils and rice, it can get thick when it cools. The best way to reheat it is to add a little water to a serving in a pot and simmer over medium-low heat until warmed through. Because you've added water, you might need to compensate for any lost flavor with a little more salt and red chile powder.

To make this dish in a 5-quart (4.74-L) slow cooker, double the ingredients and cook on high for 6 hours. A double recipe makes 14 cups (3.32 L).

Black Bean–Brown Rice *Kitchari*

SLOW COOKER SIZE: 3½ QUART (3.32 L); COOKING TIME: 4 HOURS ON HIGH; YIELD: 6 CUPS (1.42 L)

This was an experiment I tried because my younger daughter, Aria, loves black beans so much. I've never seen this combination in an Indian household, but it turned out to be delicious. I actually had to stop Aria from eating a fourth bowl because I was afraid she'd explode. Try eating this with a side of your favorite salsa.

1 cup (227 g) dried black beans, picked over and washed

½ cup (95 g) brown basmati rice, washed

½ red onion, peeled and quartered

1 (1-inch [2.5-cm]) piece ginger root, peeled and cut in pieces

4 garlic cloves, peeled and trimmed

1–2 green Thai, serrano, or cayenne chiles, stems removed, chopped

2 teaspoons Roasted Ground Cumin (see recipe on page 62)

2 teaspoons coarse sea salt

1 teaspoon turmeric powder

1 teaspoon red chile powder or cayenne

6 cups (1.42 L) water

½ cup (8 g) chopped fresh cilantro, for garnish

1. Put the beans and rice in the slow cooker. (See page 47 for details on making this dish without a slow cooker.)

2. In a food processor, process the onion, ginger root, garlic, and chiles to a watery paste. Add this mixture to the slow cooker.

3. Add the cumin, salt, turmeric, red chile powder, and water.

4. Cook on high for 4 hours. Garnish with the cilantro and serve with a side of salsa.

Try This! Mix in a few tablespoons of Cashew Cream (see recipe on page 65) to give the dish an added richness in lieu of sour cream.

To make this dish in a 5-quart (4.74-L) slow cooker, double all the ingredients and cook on high for 6 hours. A double recipe makes 13 cups (3.08 L).

"*Paneer*" Biryani

SLOW COOKER SIZE: 3½ QUART (3.32 L); COOKING TIME: 3 HOURS ON LOW; YIELD: 10 CUPS (2.37 L)

Biryani is a spiced rice and meat dish that is wildly popular in Muslim homes. Of course, meat is a big part of this meal traditionally, but the basic premise of a well-spiced dish infusing a layer of basmati rice layered on top can work with any main ingredient. I tried it with baked tofu, but you can also use seitan or tempeh. Use this recipe as a basic template to get your creative culinary juices flowing.

1 cup (237 mL) plain, unsweetened soy yogurt

1 (2-inch [5-cm]) piece ginger root, peeled and grated or minced

2 garlic cloves, peeled and grated or minced

2–4 green Thai, serrano, or cayenne chiles, stems removed, thinly sliced

1 tablespoon *garam masala*

1 tablespoon ground coriander

½ teaspoon red chile powder or cayenne

½ teaspoon turmeric powder

1 teaspoon coarse sea salt

½ cup (8 g) fresh cilantro, minced

½ cup (8 g) fresh mint, stemmed and minced

2 (14-ounce [397-g]) packages extra-firm organic tofu, baked and cubed (see the Baked, Spiced Tofu recipe on page 68) (4 cups)

2 tablespoons oil, divided

1 teaspoon cumin seeds

½ teaspoon cardamom seeds

1 teaspoon fennel seeds

2 medium onions, peeled and thinly sliced (3 cups [450 g])

1 large tomato, roughly chopped (2 cups [320 g])

2 cups (380 g) brown basmati rice cooked with 4 cups (978 mL) water (slightly al dente)

1. In a deep bowl, combine the yogurt, ginger root, garlic, green chiles, *garam masala*, coriander, red chile powder, turmeric, salt, cilantro, and mint. Mix well.

2. Add the tofu and mix again to coat.

3. In a deep, heavy pan, heat 1 tablespoon of the oil over medium-high heat.

4. Add the cumin, cardamom, and fennel. Cook until the seeds sizzle, about 30 seconds.

5. Add the onions. Cook until browned, about 2 minutes, stirring gently to prevent sticking.

6. Add the tomato. Cook until softened, about 1 minute.

7. Add this mixture to the slow cooker. (See page 47 for details on making this dish without a slow cooker.)

8. Add the marinated tofu.

9. Layer the rice on top.

10. Drizzle the remaining 1 tablespoon oil as a finishing touch over the rice and cook on low for 3 hours. Serve right out of the slow cooker as a fast, easy, and delicious one-pot meal.

To make this dish in a 5-quart (4.74-L) slow cooker, double all the ingredients and cook on low for 4 hours. A double recipe makes 19 cups (4.50 L).

Indo-Chinese Fried Rice

YIELD: 7 CUPS (1.66 L)

You might be surprised to learn that Chinese food is wildly popular in India. The cuisine has been modified to suit an Indian palate: more heat, long-grain rather than short-grain rice, and a few other key ingredients. This recipe for fried rice is a real crowd pleaser. The best part is that it works best with cold rice, so pull out your leftovers!

2 tablespoons soy sauce

2 teaspoons distilled white vinegar

½ teaspoon coarse sea salt

1 teaspoon ground black pepper

½ teaspoon ground white pepper

1–2 tablespoons Instant Chile Sauce (optional; recipe follows)

2 tablespoons sesame or peanut oil, divided

1 (2-inch [5-cm]) piece ginger root, peeled and grated or minced

3 cloves garlic, peeled and grated or minced

1 cup snow peas, cut into matchsticks

1 medium carrot, finely diced (1 cup [128 g])

1 green bell pepper, diced (1 cup [150 g])

½ small white cabbage, finely sliced (1 cup [70 g])

4 cups (760 g) cooked brown or white basmati or other long-grain rice

2 green onions, trimmed and thinly sliced, for garnish

2–4 green Thai, serrano, or cayenne chiles, stems removed, thinly sliced, for garnish

1. Make the sauce. In a small bowl, mix together the soy sauce, vinegar, salt, black and white peppers, and Instant Chile Sauce (if using).

2. In a large wok or deep, heavy-bottom pan, heat 1 tablespoon of the oil over medium-high heat.

3. Add the ginger root and garlic, allowing both to infuse the oil. Cook for a few minutes, stirring constantly to avoid burning and to prevent the mixture from sticking to the bottom of the pan.

4. Add the snow peas, carrot, bell pepper, and cabbage and cook for 2 to 3 minutes. You want the vegetables to remain crisp, so avoid overcooking. Transfer the mixture to a large bowl.

5. In the same pan, heat the remaining 1 tablespoon oil. Add the rice and cook, stirring constantly, until it hardens a tiny bit and is cooked through, 2 to 4 minutes.

6. Add the sauce to the rice and mix well. Mix in the vegetables. Garnish with the green onions and chiles and serve immediately.

Note: The beauty of this recipe is that you can substitute whatever veggies you have on hand, including green beans, bok choy, broccoli, cauliflower, baby corn, water chestnuts—just about anything.

Instant Chile Sauce

I normally dislike having to make a dish and a sauce to go with it, but this one is so easy and so worth it that I just have to share it with you. The secret to Indo-Chinese food often is the sauce. You can make this and store it in the fridge to use with all your stir-fry recipes. Keep in mind, though, it does pack some heat. I serve my girls the above recipe without the chile sauce and then add the sauce for the adults.

10 whole, dried red chiles, roughly chopped

1 green Thai, serrano, or cayenne chile pepper, stem removed

2 cloves garlic, peeled and trimmed

2 tablespoons jaggery (*gur*) or brown sugar

1 teaspoon coarse sea salt

3 tablespoons (45 mL) distilled white vinegar

2 tablespoons sesame or peanut oil

1. Soak the red chiles in boiled water to soften for about 10 to 15 minutes.

2. In a regular blender, food processor, or a more powerful blender, such as a Vitamix, combine all the ingredients except the oil and process until smooth. Transfer the mixture to a small bowl.

3. Heat the oil on the stovetop until it's very hot and add it to the sauce. Store this sauce in the fridge for up to 1 week.

Meatless Dishes, Indian Inspired

Spiced Crumbles with Peas (*Mock Keema*)

YIELD: 4 CUPS [948 ML]

It seemed almost blasphemy to make this North India comfort food vegan—it's traditionally made with lamb. But I took the chance and I'm glad I did. I've turned many a meateater (even Indian) around with this recipe—you will too!

2 (12-ounce [341-g]) bags meatless ground crumbles (such as those made by Quorn, Boca, or Morningstar)

1 large yellow or red onion, peeled and quartered

1 (2-inch [5-cm]) piece ginger root, peeled and cut into 6 pieces

8 cloves garlic, peeled and trimmed

3–6 green Thai, serrano, or cayenne chiles, stems removed

2 tablespoons oil

1 teaspoon cumin seeds

¼ teaspoon green cardamom seeds, lightly crushed

¼ teaspoon fenugreek seeds, lightly crushed

2 cassia leaves (or bay leaves)

1 teaspoon turmeric powder

2 medium tomatoes, peeled and diced (2 cups [320 g])

1 cup (237 mL) water

1 tablespoon Roasted Ground Cumin (see recipe on page 62)

1 tablespoon ground coriander

1 tablespoon coarse sea salt

1 teaspoon *garam masala*

1 heaping teaspoon red chile powder or cayenne

1 teaspoon ground black pepper

1 cup (145 g) peas, fresh or frozen

2 tablespoons chopped fresh cilantro, for garnish

1. If the ground crumbles are frozen, defrost them. Otherwise, you'll need to increase the cooking time a bit.

2. In a food processor, process the onion, ginger root, garlic, and green chiles. If you don't have a food processor, no worries! You just have to work a little harder to mince these ingredients. I would suggest mincing the onion and chiles and grating the ginger root and garlic. Then, put them all together and continue to mince with a chef's knife.

3. In a heavy, wide pan, heat the oil over medium-high heat.

4. Add the cumin seeds, cardamom, fenugreek, cassia leaves, and turmeric. Cook for 1 minute, until the seeds sizzle. Don't overcook the fenugreek, which can turn bitter.

5. Add the onion mixture. Cook for 2 minutes, stirring occasionally.

6. Add the tomatoes. Keep stirring occasionally and mashing the mixture with the back of a spoon. Cook for 3 minutes.

7. Add the water.

8. Add the ground crumbles, ground cumin, coriander, salt, *garam masala*, red chile powder, and black pepper. Reduce the heat to low or medium-low and cook for 8 to 10 minutes.

9. Add the peas. Cook for 3 minutes.

10. Garnish with the cilantro and serve with brown or white basmati rice.

Mock Egg Salad

YIELD: 2 CUPS (474 ML)

I started making this recipe back in graduate school in Hawaii in the mid-1990s. I'd eaten it at a vegetarian buffet at a temple on Oahu and was blown away by how delicious it was. I must have made it a million times since—it's that good—for potlucks on Sans Souci Beach and for my kids' lunch boxes in Chicago. Heat up a slice of toast, spread it with soy butter and Mock Egg Salad, and you'll never miss the real thing.

1 (14-ounce [397-g]) package organic extra-firm tofu

⅓ cup (50 g) diced yellow or red onion

⅓ cup (40 g) diced celery

⅓ cup (43 g) diced carrots

¼ teaspoon Roasted Ground Cumin (see recipe on page 62)

¼ teaspoon red chile powder, cayenne, or paprika

½ teaspoon coarse sea salt

½ teaspoon turmeric powder

½ teaspoon ground black pepper

¼ cup (59 mL) vegan mayonnaise

1. In a deep bowl, mash down the tofu with your hands.

2. Add the remaining ingredients and mix well with a spoon or the back of a large fork. Refrigerate for at least an hour before serving. Serve it traditionally, as a filling for a sandwich, or as a dip with veggies.

Seitan *Tikka Masala*

YIELD: 5 CUPS (1.19 L)

You'll never miss the chicken with this curry, because it's so creamy and delicious. Eat it with thick, piping hot naan *and you'll literally be in a food coma for days.*

MARINATED SEITAN:

1 cup (237 mL) plain, unsweetened soy yogurt

Juice of 1 medium lemon

1 (½-inch [13-mm]) piece ginger root, peeled and grated or minced

3 cloves garlic, peeled and grated or minced

1 heaping teaspoon paprika

1 teaspoon red chile powder or cayenne

1 teaspoon ground cinnamon

1 teaspoon ground black pepper

1 teaspoon coarse sea salt

2 (8-ounce [227-g]) packages plain, cubed seitan, rinsed (3 cups)

MASALA:

1 large yellow or red onion, peeled and quartered

3 cloves garlic, peeled and trimmed

2–4 Thai, serrano, or cayenne chiles, stems removed

1 (6-ounce [180-mL]) can tomato paste

1 tablespoon *garam masala*

1 tablespoon ground coriander

1 teaspoon red chile powder or cayenne

2 teaspoons coarse sea salt

2 teaspoons jaggery (*gur*)

1 cup (237 mL) water

3 medium tomatoes, peeled and diced (3 cups [480 g])

4 tablespoons (60 mL) oil, divided

3 green cardamom pods, slightly crushed

3 whole cloves

½ cup (119 mL) Cashew Cream (see recipe on page 65)

1. In a deep bowl, whisk together all the marinated seitan ingredients except the seitan itself.

2. Add the seitan to the marinade and mix gently until all the pieces are coated. (If there are larger pieces, slice them thin or cube them first.)

3. Let the seitan marinate while you prep the *masala*.

4. In a food processor, combine the onion, garlic, chiles, tomato paste, *garam masala*, coriander, red chile powder, salt, jaggery, and water and process until smooth.

5. Add the tomatoes to the food processor and pulse a few times until they are just broken down but not completely blended.

6. In a deep, heavy pan, heat 2 tablespoons of the oil over medium-high heat.

7. Add the onion–tomato mix, along with the cardamom and cloves, and bring to a boil. Reduce the heat and simmer for 15 minutes. Put a lid on the pan; it will splatter like spaghetti sauce as it thickens.

8. Meanwhile, in a separate frying pan, heat the remaining 2 tablespoons of oil.

9. Carefully use tongs to transfer the marinated pieces of seitan to the pan. Cook for 2 to 4 minutes on each side, browning them slightly. Turn off the heat when the seitan is finished cooking. (You can add any soy-yogurt marinade remaining in the bowl to the simmering *masala*.)

10. Once the *masala* has finished cooking, turn off the heat and add the Cashew Cream. Mix well.

11. Add the browned pieces of seitan. Replace the lid on the pan and let your dish sit for 10 minutes to let all the flavors mix. Remove the whole spices. Serve with thick *naan*, *tandoori roti*, or white or brown basmati rice. Organic extra-firm tofu or tempeh can be used in place of the seitan.

Tandoori Tempeh

YIELD: ABOUT 24 PIECES

Tandoori *paste is probably one of the most misunderstood elements of Indian cooking. Most associate it with* tandoori *chicken, which is served bright red in Indian restaurants. It's not clear how this practice started, but the red color largely comes from red food dye. Some Indian cookbook authors continue to include this dye in their recipes for* tandoori *chicken. I choose not to, especially knowing all the negative health effects of food dyes, especially on children. The principle ingredients of* tandoori *paste—yogurt, ginger root, garlic, and spices—are all you need.*

¼ (59 mL) cup water

1 (2-inch [5-cm]) piece ginger root, peeled and cubed

10 cloves garlic, peeled and trimmed

1 cup (237 mL) plain, unsweetened soy yogurt

1 teaspoon paprika

1 teaspoon red chile powder or cayenne

1 teaspoon *garam masala*

1 teaspoon dried fenugreek leaves (*kasoori methi*)

1 heaping tablespoon tomato paste

2 (8-ounce [227-g]) packages tempeh, any flavor

1. Set an oven rack at the highest position and preheat the oven to 375°F (190°C). Line a baking sheet with aluminum foil for easy clean up.

2. In a regular blender or a more powerful blender, such as a Vitamix, combine the water, ginger root, and garlic and blend to a paste.

3. Add the yogurt, paprika, red chile powder, *garam masala*, fenugreek leaves, and tomato paste and process until you have a bright, red marinade.

4. Cut the tempeh into strips about 3 inches (7.5 cm) long, 1 inch (2.5 cm) wide, and ¼-inch (6-mm) thick.

5. Pour about a third of the marinade into a shallow baking dish. Arrange the tempeh pieces in the dish. Pour another spoonful or two of marinade over the tempeh until all pieces are covered.

6. Let the tempeh marinate for at least 20 minutes and up to 2 hours.

7. Bake for 20 minutes, flipping each piece halfway through. Serve over brown or white basmati rice or as a filling for a sandwich or wrap. Organic extra-firm tofu or seitan can be used in place of the tempeh.

Tofu Curry

YIELD: 2 CUPS (474 ML)

This dish was one of my biggest surprises. The soy yogurt mixed perfectly with the spices and provided the much-needed moisture and texture that dairy yogurt does for traditional Indian curries. The tofu was an unexpectedly delicious addition, especially when baked first. You can also use unbaked tofu, but it will have a softer texture, which I liked but which did not make the cut with my more discerning husband. Make it both ways and decide for yourself.

1 small yellow or red onion, peeled and quartered

1 (2-inch [5-cm]) piece ginger root, peeled and coarsely chopped

5 cloves garlic, peeled and trimmed

1 medium tomato, quartered

2–3 green Thai, serrano, or cayenne chiles, stems removed, halved

½ cup (119 mL) plain, unsweetened soy yogurt

1 heaping teaspoon coarse sea salt

2 teaspoons *garam masala*

1 teaspoon dried fenugreek leaves (*kasoori methi*), lightly crushed in your hand to release their flavor

1 teaspoon red chile powder or cayenne

2 tablespoons oil

½ teaspoon asafetida (*hing*)

1 teaspoon cumin seeds

1 teaspoon turmeric powder

1 (2-inch [5-cm]) cinnamon stick

2 green cardamom pods (lightly crushed)

2 whole cloves

½ cup (119 mL) water

1 (14-ounce [397-g]) package extra-firm organic tofu, baked and cubed (see the Baked, Spiced Tofu recipe on page 68)

2 tablespoons chopped fresh cilantro, for garnish

1. In a food processor, process the onion, ginger root, garlic, tomato, and chiles to a smooth, slightly watery paste. Transfer the mixture to a bowl.

2. Add the yogurt, salt, *garam masala*, fenugreek leaves, and red chile powder. Mix well.

3. In a deep, heavy pan, heat the oil over medium-high heat.

4. Add the asafetida, cumin, turmeric, cinnamon, cardamom, and cloves. Cook for 30 seconds, until the seeds sizzle.

5. Add the soy yogurt mixture and the water. Bring to a boil. Reduce the heat and simmer for 10 to 15 minutes, until the mixture thickens slightly. (This step is key. The spices need to cook and blend evenly into the other ingredients.)

6. Add the tofu. Simmer for another 4 to 5 minutes. Remove the whole spices, garnish with the fresh cilantro, and serve immediately over a bed of brown or white basmati rice.

Masala Soy Granules/TVP

YIELD: 2 CUPS (474 ML)

Soy nugget curry is commonly found on North Indian dinner tables. This is an easy take on the more-common ground soy crumbles. Add your choice of veggies, and you'll have your own spin on this meat-inspired ingredient.

1 cup (85 g) textured vegetable (soy) protein (TVP)

1 cup (237 mL) boiled water

1 tablespoon oil

1 teaspoon cumin seeds

½ teaspoon turmeric powder

½ medium yellow or red onion, peeled and diced (½ cup [75 g])

1 heaping tablespoon grated peeled ginger root

½ teaspoon *garam masala*

½ teaspoon red chile powder or cayenne

1 teaspoon coarse sea salt

2 tablespoons chopped fresh cilantro

1. Put the TVP in the boiled water and let it sit for at least 5 minutes.

2. In a heavy pan, heat the oil over medium-high heat.

3. Add the cumin and turmeric. Cook until the seeds sizzle, about 30 seconds.

4. Add the onion and cook for 2 minutes, until slightly brown, stirring to avoid sticking.

5. Add the ginger root. Cook for another minute.

6. Add the soaked TVP (you won't need to drain it; it will absorb all the liquid), *garam masala*, red chile powder, and salt. Cook for 2 to 4 minutes, until your dish is dry and slightly browned.

7. Add the cilantro and serve with brown or white basmati rice, in a pita, or over tortillas.

Try This! Take about ½ cup (119 mL) of this recipe and mix it in with plain, cooked black beans, and you've got an easy, healthy, and delicious filling for a taco, tortilla, or burrito. I made it for dinner for my girls, and Neha said it was good enough to go into this book! It's seasoned well enough that you don't even need to add spices.

Black Forest Burger

One day, I found beets and kale in my fridge alongside a ton of leftover black chickpeas. The rest is history. The best part is that it's completely approved by my young girls—who would have thought that kids would be into beets and kale? Try it with your kids and see what they think.

2 cups (328 g) cooked black chickpeas (*kala chana*) or black beans

2 cups (380 g) cooked brown basmati rice

2 tablespoons oil, plus more for frying

1 cup (92 g) gram (chickpea) flour (*besan*)

½ cup (15 g) chopped kale, beet greens, or other deep green leafy vegetable

¼ cup (4 g) minced fresh cilantro

½ cup (75 g) peeled and grated uncooked yam or sweet potato

½ cup (68 g) peeled and grated uncooked beets (about 2 small)

½ cup (35 g) grated red cabbage

½ small red onion, minced

1 (1-inch [2.5-cm]) piece ginger root, peeled and grated

1 tablespoon coarse sea salt

1 tablespoon ground coriander

1 teaspoon turmeric powder

1 teaspoon red chile powder or cayenne

2 teaspoons *garam masala*

1. In a food processor, process the chickpeas or beans, rice, and 2 tablespoons of the oil until well mixed and blended. Be patient, as this could take some time. If you have a smaller processor, do this in batches. Add the gram flour ½ cup (46 g) at a time, processing after each addition. Add the greens and process until smooth. Transfer this mixture to a deep bowl.

2. Mix in the cilantro, yam or sweet potato, beets, cabbage, onion, and ginger root by hand. Add the salt, coriander, turmeric, red chile powder, and *garam masala* and mix until blended.

3. With your hands, form the mixture into small balls, flatten them into patties, and set them aside on a tray.

4. Lightly oil a griddle or frying pan and heat the patties until browned on both sides, about 4 or 5 minutes per side, over medium heat. It helps to put a lid on the pan and occasionally press down on the patties with a spatula to allow them to cook through. Alternatively, these veggie patties are hearty enough to cook on a grill. They become slightly crisp on the outside and remain soft and moist on the inside.

Try This! Laura, one of my taste testers, patted the patties with a little flour before pan-frying them to give them an added layer of crunchiness. (For a gluten-free version, try cornmeal.)

Masala Chickpea Burger

YIELD: 12 (3-INCH [7.5-CM] ROUND) BURGERS

I cannot stand frozen veggie burgers from the store. They taste like cardboard. That's precisely why my mom and I started experimenting one day in the kitchen. Making your own veggie burgers is easy and incredibly fun for the whole family. Freeze them and pull them out during the week for an easy meal. I guarantee you won't go back to prepackaged burgers again.

2 cups (328 g) cooked white chickpeas

2 cups (380 g) cooked brown rice (any kind)

1 cup (150 g) uncooked yam or sweet potato, peeled and grated

1 carrot, grated (you can also use zucchini)

½ cup (35 g) white cabbage, grated

½ small white onion, peeled and minced

1 (1-inch [2.5-cm]) piece ginger root, peeled and grated or minced

¾ cup (69 g) gram (chickpea) flour (*besan*)

1 tablespoon coarse sea salt

1 teaspoon turmeric powder

1 teaspoon red chile powder or cayenne

2 teaspoons *garam masala*

1 tablespoon ground coriander

¼ cup (4 g) minced fresh cilantro

2 tablespoons oil, plus more for pan frying

1. In a food processor, blend the chickpeas and rice until well combined.

2. Add the remaining ingredients and process again until smooth.

3. With your hands, form the mixture into small balls and flatten them into patties. If the dough is too sticky and soft, just add a little more gram flour. Set aside on a tray.

4. In a shallow frying pan, heat the oil over medium-high heat. Add the patties and heat until browned on both sides, 2 to 3 minutes per side. I like to put a lid on the pan and cook for an additional minute on each side to make sure the patties and the gram flour are cooked through. Serve on a hamburger bun with all the fixings, or on a large lettuce leaf for a lighter meal.

Masala Pizza

YIELD: 4 PITAS

During a visit to India, I ordered a pizza to get a little piece of Americana in Delhi. I was homesick for all of my friends and really didn't want to be on a family trip—typical teenager mentality. The "pizza" that came made me even more homesick. It was a layer of dough topped with an Indian curried bean dish. I was appalled. The funny thing is, now I'm making my own version of "curried" pizza and loving it! Using pita for the crust makes it a fun, fast treat during the week for the kids as well—a tip I picked up from one of my favorite magazines, Clean Eating.

4 large whole-wheat or gluten-free pitas

1 tablespoon oil

½ teaspoon cumin seeds

1 medium yellow or red onion, peeled and minced (1 cup [150 g])

4 cloves garlic, peeled and minced

4 cups (120 g) chopped greens (spinach, kale, winter greens, or a mix)

½ teaspoon coarse sea salt

1 teaspoon *garam masala*

2 tablespoons grated vegan cheese

1. Heat the pita in a toaster oven until just warm. Don't overcook it, but toasting the pita a bit helps keep it crispy later, when you add the toppings.

2. In a sauté pan, heat the oil over medium-high heat.

3. Add the cumin and cook until the seeds sizzle, about 30 seconds.

4. Add the onion and garlic and cook for 1 to 2 minutes.

5. Add the greens and cook until just wilted.

6. Add the salt and *garam masala*.

7. Divide this mixture equally among the pitas. Sprinkle each with vegan cheese.

8. Place the pitas in the toaster oven and cook just until the cheese melts. Serve immediately.

Chutneys

Mint Chutney

YIELD: 2 CUPS (474 ML)

If you love Indian food, you probably need no introduction to this chutney. But even seasoned Indian food lovers may be surprised that most North Indian families have a patch of mint growing in their backyards precisely for this purpose. It's funny that despite the fact that folks love it so much, most don't realize how incredibly easy it is to whip up.

4 cups (64 g) packed fresh mint leaves, stems removed

½ medium yellow or red onion, peeled and roughly chopped

1 (1-inch [2.5-cm]) piece ginger root, peeled and chopped

1 clove garlic, peeled and trimmed

3–6 green Thai, serrano, or cayenne chiles, stems removed

1 teaspoon coarse sea salt

1 teaspoon red chile powder or cayenne

1 teaspoon jaggery (gur) or brown sugar

Juice of 1 lemon

1. Combine all the ingredients in a regular blender, food processor, or a more powerful blender, such as a Vitamix, and process until smooth. If you want to make your chutney a little smoother, you can add 1 to 2 tablespoons of water when blending. Serve as a side for Indian meals and snacks, or do as many Indian mothers do for their little ones—make simple vegan butter and chutney sandwiches.

Mint–Cilantro Chutney

YIELD: 2 CUPS (474 ML)

A combination of mint and cilantro is used often in chutney. The cilantro tones down the mint and gives a more subtle flavor. This combination is what is most often sold in Indian grocery stores, but a jar bought there just can't match the taste of homemade.

2 cups (32 g) packed fresh mint leaves, stems removed

2 cups (32 g) packed fresh cilantro, trimmed and chopped

1 medium yellow or red onion, peeled and roughly chopped (1 cup [150 g])

1 (2-inch [5-cm]) piece ginger root, peeled and roughly chopped

2 cloves garlic, peeled and trimmed

2–3 green Thai, serrano, or cayenne chiles, stems removed

Juice of 1 lemon

1 tablespoon grated jaggery (*gur*) or brown sugar

1½ teaspoon coarse sea salt

¼ teaspoon red chile powder or cayenne

1. Combine all the ingredients in a regular blender, food processor, or a more powerful blender, such as a Vitamix, and process until smooth. Be patient when processing. At first, it will look like you'll need water, but when everything mixes together and hits the blades, it will all blend down perfectly. If you want an even smoother texture, add 1 to 2 tablespoons of water when blending.

Try This! Add 1 to 2 tablespoons Cashew Cream (see recipe on page 65) for added flavor and richness. A cup of Cashew Cream (237 mL) mixed with 1 tablespoon of this chutney is a great substitute for sour cream on a baked potato. Use a tablespoon of this mixture over each potato.

Strawberry Chutney

YIELD: 1 CUP (237 ML)

The idea for this chutney was born when I was asked to make a food sample for a strawberry festival. Folks there tasted it, and I was instantly flooded with requests to bottle it for them to purchase. I haven't quite gotten to that point just yet, but I think their response indicates that this recipe is worth a try.

1 pound (454 g) strawberries, hulled and chopped (3 cups)

2 tablespoons distilled white vinegar

⅓ cup (75 g) light brown sugar (slightly more if you like it sweeter)

1 (1-inch [2.5-cm]) piece ginger root, peeled and grated or minced

2 cloves garlic, peeled and grated or minced

3 whole cloves

1 green cardamom pod, lightly crushed

1 (3-inch [7.5-cm]) cinnamon stick

1 pinch *garam masala*

1 pinch red chile powder or cayenne

1 pinch coarse sea salt

1. In a heavy, deep pan over medium-high heat, combine all the ingredients except the salt. Bring to a boil, stirring to dissolve the sugar.

2. Reduce the heat to medium and simmer uncovered for 30 minutes. Stir occasionally to prevent sticking.

3. Add the salt, remove the whole spices, and let cool for about 20 minutes before serving. You can refrigerate this chutney for up to 2 weeks.

Note: If the strawberries are of the small, locally grown variety, I like to keep them whole. But, if they are the conventional store-bought size, I prefer to chop them up to make it easier to use the chutney as a spread.

Try This! Use the mixture as a spread with vegan butter on your favorite bread, on pancakes or waffles, or in between crêpes, or as a dollop on your favorite soy yogurt.

Peach Chutney

YIELD: 2 CUPS (474 ML)

This chutney is dedicated to my dear friend Rekha Rao, who helped me come up with the spice blends. Inspiration struck one afternoon when I was experimenting with my newly purchased serrated peeler. Rekha hates peach fuzz, and once she started using my new gadget, she couldn't control herself. When every peach on my counter was peeled, an idea was born. This chutney is light—almost airy. It's perfect paired with a flavorful savory main dish like tempeh or seitan. Or maybe over some vanilla tofu ice cream?

5 peaches, peeled and chopped (about 4 cups [875 g])

1 (1-inch [2.5-cm]) piece ginger root, peeled and grated or minced

⅓ cup (75 g) light brown sugar

2 tablespoons distilled white vinegar

1 star anise

1 heaping teaspoon ground roasted fennel seeds

2 whole dried red chiles, roughly chopped

½ teaspoon coarse sea salt

½ teaspoon red chile powder or cayenne

Juice of ½ lime

1. In a saucepan over medium-high heat, combine all the ingredients except the lime. Bring to a boil.

2. Reduce the heat to medium-low and simmer uncovered for 40 minutes. At first the peaches will release their juices, and you'll have a soupy consistency. Toward the end of your cooking time, the juices will evaporate and you'll have a more jelly-like consistency. Be sure to stir a few times to prevent sticking.

3. Add the lime juice and remove the whole spices. Serve warm or refrigerate for up to 2 weeks.

Note: To roast fennel seeds, put them in a dry, shallow pan over medium-high heat. Shake the pan back and forth over the heat until the seeds brown, as if you were toasting nuts. Transfer them to a cold plate. Let them sit for about 15 minutes before grinding.

Tomato Chutney/*Masala* "Ketchup"

YIELD: 2 CUPS (474 ML)

In India, even ketchup has a kick to it. Masala ketchups are found at most every eatery. This recipe is a fun take on ketchup that you'll enjoy with everything from veggie burgers to "eggs." It starts as a tomato chutney, and then I give it a whirl in my Vitamix blender. This basic recipe was shared with me by Mukta Gupta, who was a close friend and cooking buddy during my days as a graduate student at the University of Hawaii and East–West Center.

1 tablespoon oil

½ teaspoon cumin seeds

½ teaspoon nigella seeds (*kalonji*)

½ medium yellow or red onion, peeled and minced (¾ cup [113 g])

1 (1-inch [2.5-cm]) piece ginger root, peeled and grated or minced

2 cloves garlic, peeled and grated or minced

2 large tomatoes, peeled and diced (3 cups [480 g])

2–4 green Thai, serrano, or cayenne chiles, stems removed, chopped

2 tablespoons grated jaggery (*gur*)

1 teaspoon coarse sea salt

1 teaspoon *garam masala*

1 teaspoon ground coriander

1 teaspoon red chile powder or cayenne

Juice of 1 lemon

1. In a deep, heavy pan, heat the oil over medium-high heat.

2. Add the cumin and nigella, and cook until the seeds pop, about 30 seconds.

3. Add the onion. Cook for 2 minutes, until slightly browned.

4. Add the ginger root and garlic and cook for another 2 minutes.

5. Add tomatoes, chiles, jaggery, salt, *garam masala*, coriander, and red chile powder.

6. Bring to a boil, and reduce the heat and simmer for 5 minutes. At this point, the tomatoes will break down and the mixture will thicken slightly. Add the lemon juice. Eat as a side just like this, or try blending it.

7. If blending, add the mixture to the jug of a blender or a more powerful blender, such as a Vitamix, and blend on high until completely smooth. Serve as a side to a meal, with veggie burgers, or even with mock eggs. It's also delicious spread on toast and eaten with samosas and other Indian snacks. I'll sometimes mix it into plain, cooked brown or white basmati rice for a little added flavor.

Tamarind–Date Chutney (*Imlee Ke Chutney*)

YIELD: 2 CUPS (474 ML)

According to my mother, my grandmother (Nani) made her tamarind chutney with dates. I always love finding new ways to take out the processed sugars and add more natural sweeteners, so this recipe makes total sense. Take the time to make your own Tamarind Juice, and you'll have an even healthier version of the chutney sold in most restaurants and grocery stores.

3 cups (711 mL) Tamarind Juice (see recipe on page 66)

1 cup (147 g) dates, roughly chopped (about 15 medium)

¾ cup (150 g) jaggery (*gur*) or dark brown sugar

½ teaspoon ground ginger

½ teaspoon black salt (*kala namak*)

1 teaspoon coarse sea salt

1 teaspoon red chile powder or cayenne

1 teaspoon *garam masala*

1 teaspoon Roasted Ground Cumin (see recipe on page 62)

1. In a heavy saucepan over medium-high heat, combine the Tamarind Juice, dates, and jaggery and bring to a boil.

2. Reduce the heat and simmer for 15 minutes.

3. Either in a blender or using an immersion blender, blend the mixture. Return the mixture to a boil, and then reduce the heat and simmer again until it thickens, about 2 to 3 minutes.

4. Add the ginger, black salt, sea salt, red chile powder, *garam masala*, and cumin.

Note: If you don't have Tamarind Juice handy or don't have time to make it, dissolve 5 tablespoons (75 mL) of tamarind paste in 3 cups (711 mL) of water.

Coconut Chutney

YIELD: 2 CUPS (474 ML)

No South Indian meal is complete without coconut chutney. It's not complicated to make, but getting your hands on fresh coconuts and cracking them open might seem to be. If you can find a place that has them (my local Whole Foods Market does), just ask the produce folks to break it open for you. Remember, packaged coconut always works, too.

1 tablespoon split gram (*chana dal*)

2 cups (160 g) fresh unsweetened grated coconut

1 (1-inch [2.5-cm]) piece ginger root, peeled

1–2 green Thai, serrano, or cayenne chiles, stems removed

6–7 mint leaves, stems removed

¼ cup (4 g) fresh cilantro

1 teaspoon coarse sea salt

1 teaspoon red chile powder or cayenne

2 tablespoons Tamarind Juice (see recipe on page 66) or 1 teaspoon tamarind paste

1 cup (237 mL) water

1 tablespoon oil

1 teaspoon black mustard seeds

5–6 curry leaves, roughly chopped

3 whole dried red chiles

1. Dry roast the split gram over medium-high heat, stirring and mixing occasionally.

2. In a powerful blender, such as a Vitamix, blend the coconut, ginger root, green chiles, mint, cilantro, roasted split gram, salt, red chile powder, Tamarind Juice, and water until smooth. Transfer this mixture to a bowl.

3. In a shallow pan, heat the oil over medium-high heat.

4. Add the mustard, curry leaves, and whole red chiles and lightly brown, about 30 seconds.

5. Add this mixture to the chutney. Mix lightly. Serve as a side to any meal, especially with *dosas*.

Note: For a more traditional version, omit the mint and cilantro.

Grated Daikon with Ginger

YIELD: 2 CUPS [474 ML]

Whenever we have a meal during an Indian festival, including Diwali, my mother-in-law avoids serving onions for religious reasons. Instead, she serves this chutney, which is more like a salsa. We absolutely love it.

4 large daikon radishes, peeled, grated, and squeezed to remove any excess water

1 (2-inch [5-cm]) piece ginger root, peeled and cut into matchsticks

½ teaspoon coarse sea salt

½ teaspoon ground black pepper

Juice of 1 lemon

1. In a deep bowl, mix together all the ingredients. Serve immediately.

Hot Chile and Mustard Pickles
(Mirchi ka Achaar)

YIELD: 2 CUPS (474 ML)

One weekend, my husband and I visited my parents' home only to find there one of the best Indian pickles (achaar) we've ever tasted. The recipe is from my mother's childhood friend from India, Usha Sharma, who learned by watching her grandmother in India. It's a shame that this art of making homemade pickles is slowly dying as people opt for store-bought versions, because making a batch fresh at home only take minutes and will last you months.

2 cups (300 g) green Thai, serrano, cayenne, or habañero chiles, stems removed

2 teaspoons coarse sea salt

2 teaspoons turmeric powder

2 tablespoons ground black or yellow mustard seeds

1 teaspoon mango powder (*amchur*)

1 teaspoon *garam masala*

2 teaspoons Sucanat or other sweetener

2 tablespoons mustard oil

1. Wearing kitchen gloves, cut a slit lengthwise down each chile with a sharp knife, stopping at the stem. Be careful not to cut the chiles in half, as you'll need to stuff them later.

2. In a bowl, combine the salt, turmeric, ground mustard, mango powder, *garam masala*, and Sucanat. Mix well.

3. Stuff each individually with this mixture (wear gloves if you need them).

4. In a heavy pan, heat the mustard oil over medium-high heat.

5. Add the stuffed peppers. Cook, stirring constantly, for 2 minutes.

6. Turn off the heat and remove the pan from the burner.

7. Add the leftover *masala* and mix gently. Let the peppers sit for 15 minutes.

8. Transfer to an airtight glass jar. Place the jar in a cool place with the lid off and let the mixture cool completely, at least 2 to 4 hours.

9. Seal the container and store in the refrigerator. Enjoy the Pickles as a condiment with any Indian meal, bread, or rice. We especially love it with sweet dishes like *mitha poora*.

Drinks

These are just few of my favorites. Some are traditionally Indian, but others are smoothies that I make on a daily basis. Many of you have asked me for my recipes, so here they are.

Anupy's *Masala Chai*

YIELD: 4½ CUPS (1.07 L)

I'm sorry, but no one makes a better chai *than I do. The key is in limiting the sugar and including a subtle amount of cloves. Fresh ginger root adds that extra punch.*

4 cups (978 mL) water

4 green cardamom pods

1 black cardamom pod

2 whole cloves

½ teaspoon fennel seeds

1 (3-inch [7.5-cm]) cinnamon stick

1 (1-inch [2.5-cm]) piece ginger root, peeled and sliced

2 black tea bags

½ cup (119 mL) milk (soy, rice, hemp, or almond)

2 teaspoons agave nectar or other sweetener

1. In a pot, bring the water to a boil.

2. In a mortar and pestle, lightly grind the cardamom pods and cloves.

3. Add this mixture to the boiling water, along with the fennel, cinnamon stick, ginger root, and tea bags.

4. Boil for 2 to 3 minutes, until the water darkens.

5. Remove and discard the tea bags and ginger root.

6. Add the milk and bring to a boil again.

7. Add the sweetener. Mix well and serve piping hot in mugs.

Note: If you are using preground *chai masala*, use 1 teaspoon in place of the spices and ginger root.

Mattu Massi's Cold Coffee

YIELD: 2 CUPS (474 ML)

My favorite food memory is of my mother's youngest sister and her smooth, cold, and frothy cold coffee. We'd be visiting my grandmother's home in Chandigarh, and after a morning of eating and resting we'd cleanse our palates with a freshly blended glass of pure magic. It's a refreshing change to the overly sweetened cold coffees found in coffee shops in the United States. Massi uses whole dairy milk, but I substituted soy milk, and it actually worked. If you don't like soy milk, try other vegan milk substitutes.

1 cup (237 mL) unsweetened soy milk (or other nondairy milk of your choosing)

1 teaspoon instant coffee

1 tablespoon plus 1 teaspoon agave nectar or other sweetener

10 large ice cubes

1. Combine all the ingredients in a regular blender or a more powerful blender, such as a Vitamix, and blend until smooth and frothy. Serve immediately.

Green Juice Smoothie

YIELD: 8 CUPS (1.90 L)

Imagine getting all of your daily greens and fruit in one glass. This is the way! It's the one recipe I make virtually every day. It's like liquid, green gold for your body. A lot of people talk about the benefits of drinking green juice; this one is not only good for you but tastes delicious, too, with the combination of lime and ginger root. The original recipe comes from the folks at the Vitamix company, but with a few key changes, I've made it my own. Of course, having a powerful blender like a Vitamix is key to really grind everything down, but you can also make this combination in a juicer. If you have a regular blender and want to try this recipe, just pare back a little on the vegetables or cut them into pieces before adding them.

½ cup (119 mL) apple juice

½ cup (50 g) seedless green grapes

½ medium apple, unpeeled

½ medium orange, peeled

1 banana, peeled

½ cup (83 g) pineapple

½ medium carrot

½ medium cucumber with skin

2 cups (60 g) packed greens (spinach, kale, or a mix)

1 (2-inch [5-cm]) piece ginger root, peeled and cut into pieces

1 lime, peeled

1 tablespoon chia or flax seeds

2 cups (474 mL) ice cubes

3 cups (711 mL) water

1. Combine all the ingredients in a blender in the order listed. Blend for at least 2 minutes on the highest setting until you have a delicious, smooth, and frothy green drink.

Note: This juice can be stored, refrigerated, for 1 day. I typically will transfer it to a glass jar. Store it any longer, and it does become a bit rancid. Drink this juice daily, and you'll be amazed how clear your skin will become and how you'll avoid minor colds and coughs. My girls love it as well. If you don't want so much fruit, just reduce it and substitute other greens.

Blueberry–Green Smoothie

YIELD: 4 CUPS (948 ML)

Everyone thinks I'm crazy when I tell them I mix karela *and spinach with blueberries. Try it. You'll barely taste the greens. My kids love this smoothie with just the spinach—even after I finally admitted to them that they'd just gotten their daily dose of veggies along with it. Add the* karela *for you and the added health benefits.*

1 cup (155 g) frozen blueberries

1 cup (237 mL) milk (soy, almond, rice, or hemp)

1 (1-inch [2.5-cm]) piece bitter melon (*karela*) (or a handful of spinach or kale)

1 banana, peeled

2 tablespoons flax seeds

1 tablespoon chia seeds

4 almonds (preferably soaked overnight)

1 cup (237 mL) water, coconut water, or juice

2 heaping cups (474 mL) ice

1. Blend all the ingredients together until smooth, preferably in a powerful blender, such as a Vitamix. Serve immediately and enjoy getting your fruit and veggies in one shot! I do refrigerate leftovers, but they tend to only keep for about a day.

Note: Bitter melon tastes just like its name sounds—bitter. But it's an incredible ingredient to add to your diet, as it helps cleanse the blood and ease stomach problems and a variety of other ailments. I use it sparingly when serving this smoothie to my kids.

Red Velvet Smoothie

YIELD: 4 CUPS (948 ML)

This combination with strawberries, beets, and goji berries was something that came to me while running by Lake Michigan one morning. I was trying to figure out what vegetable would complement the bright red of the strawberries. I happened to have beets in the fridge already, so it made total sense. And what I created was a delicious and healthy smoothie that even my kids love.

1 cup (150 g) frozen strawberries

1 cup (237 mL) milk (soy, almond, rice, or hemp)

1–2 cups (237–474 mL) water, coconut water, or juice

1 banana, peeled

1 small beet, washed and trimmed (no need to peel)

2 tablespoons flax seeds

1 tablespoon chia seeds

2 heaping tablespoons dried goji berries

4–6 almonds (preferably soaked)

2 heaping cups (474 mL) ice

1. Blend all the ingredients together until smooth, preferably in a powerful blender, such as a Vitamix. Serve immediately and enjoy getting your fruit and veggies in one shot! I do refrigerate leftovers, but they tend to only keep for about a day.

Acknowledgments

One evening a week before the manuscript for this book was due, my two girls and I paused on the bottom step leading to their rooms and took a collective deep breath just before their bedtime. It had been a tumultuous day for me. The hours I'd had to myself while they were in school had been spent revamping recipes and writing like crazy. School pickup had been fast and furious, and dinner had been something thrown in a bowl over rice. I felt pretty guilty.

"As soon as this book is done—which is only days away—we'll have all the time in the world to ourselves. We'll do whatever you want. Dinner. Play. You name it."

My then-six-year-old, Aria, looked me straight in the eye and dejectedly said, "Yeah. But then you'll just write another book, and then another one, and then another one after that!"

My nine-year-old, Neha, ever practical, looked at her and exclaimed, "What's wrong with that? At least we'll be in it!"

This book is dedicated to my amazing and talented girls who gave up play dates, perfect spelling tests, and time with their mom for this book. Writing a cookbook is not about the fuss while promoting it; it's about the hours upon hours upon hours writing in solitude and recipe testing like crazy. It's about the time you spend away from your family and friends, ironically enough, to write a "family-style" cookbook.

It's a good thing my family had been there for me all along to help test and tweak all my recipes. The feedback they gave me along the way was invaluable.

Sandeep, I want to thank you for being my husband, friend, and business partner. All the running around and scrambling was so worth it because we did it together.

As for my mother, I must thank her for sending me recipes along the way. Even when she was in India visiting family, she would diligently write them down and email them to me. Despite her cultural resistance to doing so, she's become quite a talented recipe writer. I can just hear her asking my aunts to be more specific with measurements and steps for recipes they've likely never written down before.

I've learned a lot since I wrote my first book, *The Indian Slow Cooker*. The key thing I learned is that my mother and my family have given me a unique gift—the love and understanding of good, wholesome, plant-based foods. Not everyone can say they grew up with this in their lives. My goal is to share this gift, which I've taken for granted all these years, with all of you.

I realized the value in sharing over the last year as my inbox and Facebook page filled with notes from strangers (some of whom are now my friends) from around the country who tried some of the recipes from my first book and helped me test recipes for this book—and couldn't believe how easy and delicious they all were. I want to thank all of these people—people who I have yet to meet! There's Heather in St. Louis, author of the blog Get Skinny, Go Vegan, whose regular visits to her local Indian grocery are singlehandedly revitalizing the Indian grocery market! There's Subadra Varada-rajan in Arizona, Sally Harris in Texas, and Kip Crosby and his wife in California. Carey Montserrat in Brooklyn, who wrote to me several times a week, sadly passed away while I was writing this book. I never met you, Carey, but you touched me with your passion for good, healthy food. The list goes on and on.

I haven't even gotten to the dozens upon dozens of people in Chicago who have taste-tested for me and the personal friends around the country who have supported me every step of the way: JinJa Birkenbeuel; Rekha Rao; Raakhee Mirchandani Singh; Jasmine Narula; James Townsend; Lizabelle Russell; Elizabeth Eccher; Priti Purohit; Vanky and Nav Chandel; Inge van Reese; Amy Kartheiser; Robin Moncrieff; Miss Salvage, Miss Izzo, and Mr. Kelly (my kids' amazing teachers); Suzanne Rampage; Andrea McGinty (co-owner of Native Foods Cafe, one of the best new vegan restaurant chains in the country); Liz Ware; Mariya Shatsky; Karen Lurie; Jill Houk; and Jasmine Jafferali-Whitehead, to name just a few.

Thank you all from the bottom of my heart for your thoughtful and always gracious feedback on all the things I fed you over the last year. I know some of you still have my containers—keep them to fill with the next round of testing!

I also want to thank everyone who has given me a chance. Over the last year, I've taught classes and signed books for the best: World Kitchen in Chicago; Whole Foods Market; Sur La Table; Cost-co; the Kids' Table; the Cookbook Store in Toronto; the Olive Tap in Long Grove, Illinois; In the Kitchen in Pittsburgh; the Housewares Show in Chicago; and Good Taste! Pittsburgh, among oth-

ers. The common denominator at all these places was people who were willing to take a chance on a foodie-reporter-turned-author and said yes when I or my publisher asked.

Judith Dunbar-Hines, your sage advice and guidance has been invaluable every step of the way. I truly appreciate your willingness to be forthright and honest—it shows me how much you care. Cindy Karp, Tammy Brawley, Fanny Cantero, Alison Fryer, Elena Marre, Brian Thomas, Annette Kraus, Rick Petrocelly, Mia Rampersad, Laiza Altaf, Susan Marzano, Dee Weinberg, and Lois White with *Better Homes and Gardens*—thank you all from the bottom of my heart. Richard Harvey, thank you for replying to a random email and opening an important door for me at a very critical time in my career. And Peri Wolfman, I'll never forget you for that introduction. I never forget a favor, or that I still owe you one. Alka and Vivek Mittal—thank you for making the connections in India. You will get your 22-karat gold spice tiffin soon!

A huge thank you to my mentor, Kantha Shelke, who showed me that South Asian women can and should dare to shine.

The team at Brave New Pictures—Dave and Kathy Monk and Gregg Lowe—you, along with food stylist Mary Valentin, once again made this book shine with your impressive photography.

Special thanks to U.K.-based travel agency Trip Feast for the remarkable food tour they organized in India, leading to many of the pictures taken and used in this book. The places we stayed and visited were hands down amazing, including Ayesha Manzil, Spice Village, Chittoor Palace, and Vembanad House.

Last but not least, I'd like to thank my publisher. Doug Seibold, you took a chance on my first book and the concept for this one. My recipes, coupled with your vision and your team's persistence, made it all work. Eileen Johnson, Perrin Davis, Zach Rudin, and everyone else at the Agate office—you are truly wonderful at what you do. I am so grateful to have you all on my team. I think you'd agree that we've all learned a lot in the last year. I hope we continue to do so together.

Index

Italicized page numbers indicate photographs.

Mushrooms in Cashew Cream Sauce,
188, *189*
Mustard seed(s)
about, 35
Potato Hash, 161

N

Naan, 39
Namak (white salt), 36
Narial (coconut), 37
Nigella seeds (*kalonji*), 35
Nondairy milk, 40
North Indian
Curried Beans or Lentils, 139
Ginger Soup Stock (*Adarak
Masala*), 64
Hummus, 132
Tomato Soup (*Tamatar ka Shorba*),
87
Tomato Soup Stock (*Gila Masala*),
63
Nutmeg (*jaiphal*), 35
Nutritional yeast, 40

O

Oil, 40
Onions (*pyaz*)
about, 40
Salad, Tomato, Cucumber, and
(*Kachumber*), 113
Orange Salad, 121

P

Pakka Kela ki Sabji (*Sneh Massi's* Ripe
Banana Curry), 184
Palak "*Paneer*," (Spiced Spinach with
"*Paneer*"), 175
Panchratna Dal (Five Lentil Stew), 150
"*Paneer*" Biryani, 200

Pans, 45–46
Papad, 93
Paprika (*deghi mirch*), 30
Parantha, 39
Peach Chutney, 222
Peas
Cooked, Plain Black-Eyed (*Sookha
Lobhia*), 130
and "*Paneer*," Spiced (Mattar
"*Paneer*"), 158, *159*
Pigeon (*toor dal, toovar, arhar*, and
tur), 52
Spiced Crumbles with (*Mock
Keema*), 205
Yellow split, 52
Pickle, Indian (*achaar*), 35, 41–42
Pomegranate
Chaat, 119
seeds, about, 35
Poori, 39
Potato-Stuffed Bread (*Aloo ka
Parantha*), 72
Pots, 45–46
Pressure cookers, 21
Pudina, podina (mint), 40
Pulao (Spiced Veggie Brown Rice), 193
Punjabi
Curried Beans (*Rajmah*-Inspired
Curry), 143
Curried Lima Beans, 148, *149*
Khardi (Chickpea Flour Curry with
Veggies), 162
-Style Cabbage (*Band Gobi*), 164,
165
Pyaz (onions), 40

Q

Quickie *Masala* Beans or Lentils, 138

R

Rai (mustard seeds), 35
Rajmah-Inspired Curry (Punjabi
Curried Beans), 143
Rasam
masala, 34
Powder, 61
South Indian Tomato and
Tamarind Soup, 90
Rava Dosa (Cream of Wheat Crêpes),
80
Red Velvet Smoothie, 233
Rice (*chawal*)
about, 42
and Adzuki Bean *Dhokla*, 122, *123*
Brown, Split Gram and (*Chana Dal
Kitchari*), 198
Cumin (*Jeera Chawal*), 191
Fennel Brown (*Saunf Chawal*), 192
Indo-Chinese Fried, 201
Kitchari, Black Bean–Brown, 199
Lemon Brown, 194, *195*
and Lentil Porridge (Healing
Kitchari), 197
"*Paneer*" Biryani, 200
Spiced Veggie Brown (*Pulao*), 193
Tamarind Brown, 196
Roasted
cumin (*Bhuna hua jeera*), 31, *33*
Eggplant Dip (*Baingan Bharta*), 102
Ground Cumin (*Bhuna hua Jeera*),
62
Masala Beans or Lentils, 134
Masala Cauliflower and Broccoli
with Tomatoes, 99
Masala Nuts, 96
Rolling pin, 46

About the Author

ANUPY SINGLA was a television reporter for Chicago-based and Tribune-owned station CLTV for years before giving it all up to cook. She was determined to learn how to make every Indian recipe she grew up with, from sweet to savory, in a quest to reconnect with her Indian roots and teach her young daughters to appreciate wholesome and healthy Indian food. She blogs about her experiences at www.indianASapplepie.com. Her food-related writing has appeared in the *Chicago Sun-Times*, the *Chicago Tribune*, and the *Wall Street Journal*. Anupy is an award-winning journalist who has also reported for Bloomberg News and WGN-TV. She has a master's degree in Asian Studies from the East–West Center and the University of Hawaii, and also worked on Capitol Hill as a legislative aide. She cooks and writes from her Lincoln Park home in Chicago, where she also teaches kid and adult cooking classes for Whole Foods Market, Williams-Sonoma, and the city of Chicago's World Kitchen.